De

Dear Son is made possible in part by
a generous donation from
First Christian Church (DOC)
of Colorado Springs, Colorado,
where Jonathan Hall serves as
its Senior Pastor.

Dear Son:

Raising Faithful, Just, and Compassionate Men

Jonathan B. Hall and Beau T. Underwood

Foreword by Jim Wallis

chalice
press

Saint Louis, Missouri

ChalicePress.com

Print 9780827206786
EPUB 9780827206793
EPDF 9780827206809

Contents

Starting a Conversation on Being a Dad

by Jim Wallis

That's what this book is: Conversations about what it means to be a Dad. I am happy to start the conversation with this forward. Conversations are about questions, so here are some of the questions about being a Dad that are important to me.

"So, what do you do?"

That is a question we all get asked these days. At social events, schools, sports games, community gatherings of all kinds and is even asked in our churches. Indeed, the question most often asked of parents is what they do "for a living."

The question is mostly asked of men. It's true that women also get asked the question more and more these days. Most Moms I know work these days. According to the Labor Dept, near 3/4 of women with children under 18 worked in 2020. Non-working moms just aren't the norm anymore. But still in these community social gatherings, it is assumed that women with kids have a primary commitment to being a Mom; while that's not as clear for the men in the room. And while the men in the room as assumed to be the dads of some of the kids there, what else the men do is the question many people have. In other words, the *careers* of the men in the room can seem more important than their *vocations* as fathers.

Yet, being a Dad is the reason why all the men showed up at the event, be it a ballgame or a parent-teacher's conference, or school related party. But personally, I have found it very refreshing and even freeing to answer the common question by being able just to say that I'm "Luke's Dad" or "Jack's Dad," instead of recounting all my work outside of these gatherings. For me, my work is not really career, but a vocation; but still, it's more enjoyable to point to one of my sons in the room and say, "I'm his Dad," and that is part of my vocation.

Most of the greatest joys in our life have to do with being Moms and Dads and yet the question most often asked is about what we do. Doesn't that seem backwards to you? This book is about answering the common question with the Dad identity first, instead of the work identity first, especially when your kids are the whole reason that you are all together in the social gathering where the question gets asked.

But perhaps the most important question about being a Dad is how you spend your time. It's not how you talk about fatherhood but how take the time to do it. What I've learned is that how you treat your time in relationship to your children—for me, my two sons—is the most important question of all. Is being a Dad what you do in your "spare time" time, around the edges? Or is it time that you set aside, put ahead of other things, and make a first priority? Especially for men who are public figures—and many of us are public in some arena—kids often get relegated to the time that is left over—which means you children become left-overs too.

Being a Dad can also be regarded as a discipline—let's even say a spiritual discipline—like prayer, meditation, reading Scripture, or being alone with God. From fatherhood, you can often learn many of the same lessons that we gather from the more traditional spiritual traditions. Spiritual disciplines will never succeed or be sustained if they are just for our "extra time" and the same goes for parenthood. The cost is too great for our relationship to God or to those little human gifts that God has given to us. Setting aside *focused* time for both spiritual and family disciplines is the only way to being a genuine person of faith or being a good Dad.

For me and my family, baseball became a big part of our family discipline and the bonding. I was a Little League baseball coach for 22 seasons, over 11 years, for both of my boys. You simply can't do that in your left-over times. Both practices and games occur at the same times week in and week out and you have to build the rest of your schedule around *those times*—and not the other way around. Friday evenings and Saturdays were for us the regular baseball times. Of course, there were other times during the week that we spent together, but these baseball times were fixed, expected and reliable. So, for me, it meant no traveling and speaking on Fridays and Saturdays—period—during baseball season, which was both fall and spring.

What this offered to me and my boys was dependable time, bonding time, fun time, growing time, friendship and team building time, character formation time and lessons of life teaching times—which baseball is very good at! Not only did my time as a coach with my boys make us close, but it also got me close to their best friends and teammates, and even the parents of their teammates, which also served to bring me and my sons closer together.

Who is your most important *audience* is also a key question. I've had lots of audiences over these many years but, at some time along the way, I realized that my most important audience—meaning the people I get a chance to influence and shape—was my own children.

After every baseball game, I would always take our team away from the crowd for a post-game meeting—to share what we learned about the game, about baseball, about being a team, and even about ourselves as young men and women, and what it means to become leaders. The parents, who had to wait until the meetings were over, were often chuckling and sometimes referred these meetings as my post-game "sermons," though they were about getting the players to talk and not just me. In those precious conversations, we learned together about our talents and gifts, playing and looking out for each other and not just ourselves, serving and even sacrificing for the team, or what I call the "common good" in my work life, learning leadership skills and lessons, and believing in the power of hope. Being a part of countless teams with my sons, brought us closer together. And I have stayed in touch with many of the young men and women that I have coached—who became an audience of young adults.

This book is meant to spark conversations about fatherhood, about being a Dad. This is just a forward to that conversation, and I am very glad just to be a part of it. Listen now to Beau and Jonathan — two men who want to be good dads — to help you get this important conversation going in your own lives. I hope that one day you will feel what I feel about having kids: that being a Dad is the most important thing in my life.

Introduction

We are not perfect dads. We do not claim to be. Nor is this book intended as a guide to being a dad. While we hope to raise our sons well, we are not putting ourselves forward as exemplars. We know there's more than one way to be a father and to raise a son. We know that family circumstances are unique, and that life unfolds differently for every parent and child.

Our intention is simpler yet more profound: We want each father to reflect on what it means to have a son that calls them the weighty name of "Dad." Rather than teaching what fatherhood should be, we want to challenge each dad to make fatherhood their own. Do not uncritically accept what others tell you. Do not simply follow convention. Do not let the days and years go by without making them your own, without being the type of dad you want to be.

Our hope for this book is not only to spark a conversation about what it means to be a dad. Rather, it is to share a model of writing letters to our son(s). Letter writing is an almost lost art that we think is worth revisiting, as many find fatherhood to be daunting, lonely, and without a clear path. This way of communicating allows the writer to record their thoughts at a single moment in time to revisit in the future. It is a way to talk across the years by capturing wisdom and expressing love. It is one way of facilitating the father-son bond whose strength can last for a lifetime.

Each chapter that follows covers a different topic with a separate reflection from each of us. In reading our thoughts, you will see that our own approaches often contrast because of our different backgrounds, social locations, and personality quirks. Though our approaches might differ, our letters are all honest, authentic reflections about being dads. We believe that raising our boys to be faithful, just, and compassionate men has the capability to change the world and better reflect God's Purpose for it. We imagine you believe that too.

We want to encourage you to do the same. This book is not just meant to be read, but to be engaged with. At the close of each chapter you will find pages ready for your words and reflections. Having read our thoughts and stories on a topic, we invite you to write your own. By modeling our way of contemplating this special role, we want this book to help you become a better, more reflective dad.

We find the tradition of adding your story to an unfolding and enfolding story to be our experience with scripture. Take the example of the first canonical gospel, Mark. It has multiple endings. In fact, if you have a Study Bible, you will see comments on this. Many scholars believe that the original ending of Mark was 16:8—the women being afraid, fleeing the tomb, and not telling a single person about what had happened. Later, other people added their experience of the resurrected Christ to the end of Mark's Gospel.

We've written our book in the same manner. Rather than it being "The Final Word on Raising Faithful Boys," we are just beginning a conversation. We hope that you will add your unique story to ours. In the end, may we all experience the hope of the resurrection in the process!

If you are someone who thrives on structure, then consider using this book in a disciplined way. Commit to reading one chapter a week and then setting aside some time to write your own letter to your son. After eight weeks, you will probably think of new topics and continue the practice of writing long after the reading is done.

* * *

Since we are asking you to invest time reading our thoughts on fatherhood, you deserve to know a little bit about us and why we wrote this book.

Both of us are ministers within a denomination called the Christian Church (Disciples of Christ). Our career paths have taken us to a variety of places. We have pastored churches in places as different as California, Colorado, Missouri, and Washington, D.C. One of us (Jonathan) learned about global Christianity by studying at the Ecumenical Institute in Bossey, Switzerland. The other (Beau) has worked for progressive faith-based advocacy organizations in this nation's capital.

Regardless of the stops along our vocational journeys, one constant has been our friendship. We first met in college while serving in a leadership role with a denominationally-sponsored student ministry. Recognizing common interests and personalities, we became fast friends.

We have never lived in the same place. Our college selves could not have imagined all the twists and turns our lives would take, but we are grateful for each other's presence, camaraderie, and support along the way.

A new chapter began in each of our lives the moment our son(s) were born. Just as we moved along parallel tracks through college, seminary, and our careers in ministry, having kids at similar points became another shared experience that sparked conversation. This book was born out of our common wonder and joy at raising boys.

We pray our words will prove encouraging and inspiring to you. Your choosing to read them is heartening to us.

—*Jonathan & Beau*

1

The Joy of Fatherhood

Dear Son,

"A miracle," wrote the playwright George Bernard Shaw, "is an event that creates faith."[1] Jesse, your arrival in this world sparked joy and stirred hope in my life. It expanded my sense of what is possible and deepened my trust in the God who makes this all possible. You, my son, are a miracle.

Using miraculous language to describe the birth of a child borders on the trite. Plus, this depiction is wrong. Miracles are events that violate the laws of nature. Generating offspring is the quintessential biological task. Organisms exist to reproduce. Teachers describe to awkward, giggling teenagers during health class the lack of supernatural intervention required. By definition, there is nothing miraculous going on here.

Still, I refuse to believe it. Science may explain your physical existence but something more was involved. The explanations of textbooks cannot capture all the meaning that bursts forth when we enter the world. These events are far more expansive than what biology has to tell us. The birth of a child is an inflection point. What happens in that single moment forever changes everything that follows.

---

[1] Harold Bloom, *George Bernard Shaw's Saint Joan* (New York: Chelsea House Publishers, 1987).

Your mom and I know this truth firsthand. Alongside so many figures in the Hebrew Bible, we were forced to imagine a future without you. Our dreams of starting a family prompted a move across the country. We bought the big house, with the large fenced-in yard, in confidence that a baby would soon follow. But, like Abraham and Sarah, like Isaac and Rebekah, like Jacob and Rachel, we found ourselves lamenting the absence of a child.

We spent several years trying to get pregnant, with no success. At first we assumed patience was the only thing required, but the elapsing of months brought a strange kind of desperation. While not old, we also were not young. The ticking of the proverbial clock—an expression I now hate for its torturous images of our lives passing by and opportunities being lost — prompted us to seek help.

The biblical matriarchs and patriarchs could not have imagined the options available to us today. While I hated the idea of our bodies becoming sites of scientific experimentation, I welcomed the introduction of medical expertise. Something wasn't working with our bodies and we realized that by ourselves we weren't going to identify either the problem or a solution. Perhaps our miracle would arrive in the form of a physician.

Unfortunately, the fertility doctor was a difficult pill to swallow. He was my first encounter with someone manifesting a "God complex." We walked into the office and found his ego displayed on the wall in the form of as a mosaic of baby pictures from successful pregnancies. His message was clear: "I can make this happen for you, too." He may have meant it as reassurance, but it only increased my sense of insecurity and inadequacy. Everyone on that wall had succeeded where we, so far, had failed. At that time, he was the only fertility specialist in our area. We endured his arrogance as we moved through a battery of tests and drug regimes. Unfortunately, nothing seemed to change except the depths of our despair.

Our focus shifted to starting a family in a different way. We entered the adoption process. Offering a future to a child whose horizons might otherwise be limited counteracted the disappointment nesting within us. The social worker told us that a match would happen within a year. The nine months of anticipation during a pregnancy transformed into a twelve month gauntlet of meetings, home visits, reference checks, and other steps, but the result promised to be the same. Emotionally we wrestled with accepting this altered vision of how our family would take shape, but nonetheless excitement arose within us about this prospect.

Then, the unexpected occurred. Holiday travel made continuing the fertility treatments practically impossible, so we gave them up until January and set off for an extended California vacation. I enjoyed the ocean views and the amenities of our resort. Your mom spent the trip with a stomach that was constantly unsettled. We dared to wonder and wish what it might portend but, given the diagnosed infertility and the pausing of treatment, mostly dismissed the possibility.

We returned home to freezing temperatures and a hefty bill in the mail from the adoption agency, which had to be paid for the process to move forward. Before writing the check, your mom took a pregnancy test; and then another; and then another. To our shock and surprise, you were on the way. I was going to be a dad! Suddenly we knew the experience of the biblical patriarchs and matriarchs in a different way. Our dashed hopes for the future promised by a child were suddenly renewed.

As we began spreading our news, other dads relayed their own experience of fatherhood to me. Sometimes in a hushed whisper, as if they were disclosing a family secret, and at other times with great exclamation, as if they wanted the entire world to hear, they would say things like: "Your life is going to change in the most amazing way!" and "The world will never look the same again!"

I nodded in agreement, and would say things like "oh, I know" or "for sure." But inside I had my doubts. Those doubts had nothing to do with my excitement about becoming a dad. I was as enthusiastic as one could be, but I tend to be a realist. Even the most wonderful things have their drawbacks. These dads were acting like raising a son never involved smelly diapers/ nappies, temper tantrums, growing pains, challenging conversations, and all the fears that come with bringing a child into an uncertain and dangerous world. They made their declarations with a confidence that bordered on hyperbole. In our experience, such emphatic claims rarely held true.

These confident exclamations reminded me of late night infomercials I watched as a kid. My parents—your grandparents— bought a 12-inch Zenith TV for my bedroom one Christmas. It cost a small fortune relative to the price of televisions today, but it meant my insomnia would no longer disrupt their sleep. Instead, I would lie awake at night flipping through channels until something captured my attention. This was long before the advent of Internet streaming and TV-on-demand, and we only had basic cable, which meant my viewing options at such a late hour were quite limited.

I would frequently end up watching an infomercial for the latest, greatest product. If I would just rush to the phone (this was also long before the days of online shopping) and set up three easy payments on a credit card (promised the person making the pitch) my life would change forever. Here was a form of salvation. There was a problem from which we needed to be rescued. Deliverance was available but we needed to "Call right now!"

This logic never made sense to me. If the product was so ingenious, then why were they paying for air time at 2 a.m. on channel 4? Why wouldn't stores choose to stock it, and why wasn't it flying off their shelves? If the offer was so good, then why did they need to sweeten the deal ("But wait...there's more!") to convince people to buy? The reality rarely matched the hype.

I wondered whether fatherhood would prove to be the same. I feared that the heightened expectations others had created would lead to inevitable disappointment as the day-to-day stress of parenting overshadowed the ecstasy everyone guaranteed was coming my way.

Thankfully, my skepticism was unfounded. Becoming and then being a dad has exceeded those assurances from the other dads—and then some.

Indeed, the moment you were born is one I will never forget. After your mom and the medical team did all the hard work of bringing you into the world, seconds later I got to lay my eyes on you. Despite my usual stoicism, those eyes suddenly filled with moisture. I tried to hide my tears of happiness because there was still so much action happening in that hospital room.

The doctor and the nurses were yelling out directions, as a whirlwind of activity overtook a space that had instantly trans-formed into a nursery. Your mom was still going through the birthing process, with all the intensity and pain involved. I just stood there, next to the bed, overwhelmed by emotion. I was crying uncontrollably. Something miraculous had happened.

My joy at first seeing you is hard to express in words. In an instant, my entire world changed. My reasons for living had expanded and deepened. You were here, dependent upon your mother and me. We entered the hospital as a family of two and left as a family of three. I recall strolling by the nurses' station as we departed and waiting for them to stop us from leaving. Part of me could not believe we got to take you home. The other part of me could not believe they trusted us to keep you alive! But we quickly got over the imposter syndrome and on with the business of parenting. We left with a profound sense of purpose caused by your newfound presence among us.

As a pastor, one of my annual roles is preaching a sermon on Christmas Eve or Christmas Day. I stand up before a bunch of Christians to address what the shepherds call "this thing that has happened" (Luke 6:15 NIV). Some preachers live for this moment, but frankly I find it daunting. My task is to say something captivating and meaningful about a story the congregation knows almost by heart. They may conflate the different versions in Matthew and Luke, but they're familiar with how the events unfolded.

Except that they do not really understand it at all. None of us do. The story seems familiar on the surface, but when you dive a little deeper, the whole thing becomes unfathomable. The main claim is that God became like us in Jesus Christ. We call this the "Incarnation." Christians believe that, in the Incarnation, God came to be with us, but that idea is so exotic that our words are not as coherent as they sound. The most appropriate response we can offer to this astounding thing God has done is awe. On many occasions, I have been tempted to stand silently in the pulpit and just stare at the nativity scene with my mouth agape. My gawking would nicely convey the message. "Here is God!" announce the angels. Other than stunned surprise, is there any response that is appropriate?

Rather than preaching that stirring message in such a silent fashion, my words—and I presume that of many other pastors—usually dwell not on the metaphysics of God's arrival but on the implications that arrival or advent has for our lives. God is here! Now, what do we do? The obvious answer is take notice, change your ways accordingly, and experience the abundant life being offered.

To be clear, I would never liken you to the Christ child. You may be my perfect son but none of us is a perfect human. Plus, I want to keep your ego in check for all the discussions we are destined to have down the proverbial road. Still, there's an analogy between the birth of Jesus and welcoming a baby of your own. Your priorities have to change dramatically. Being a parent calls you to a new way of denying yourself and living for someone else.

To be your dad has required significant sacrifices. There are books left unread, ball games that went unwatched, and a lot of money spent on things I never would have bought for myself.

Those costs are real but I have no regret about them. Love and joy motivated every expense and sacrifice.

The comparison to the Christian life runs even deeper. For too many people, the biggest obstacle to following Jesus is what they perceive having to give up. As G.K. Chesterton, the philosopher and theologian, once wrote: "The Christian ideal has not been tried and found wanting. It has been found difficult; and left untried." Those intrigued by Christian faith realize their lives will have to change. The costs appear quite high, so some people decide to forego the adventure. This emphasis on the burdens of being a disciple fails to account for any of the benefits. The sacrifice may be significant but the sheer blessing that comes with the experience is incalculable.

Julian of Norwich, the mystical writer from the Middle Ages, claimed that "the fullness of joy is to behold God in everything."[2] Her exhortation reverses, yet compliments, scripture's promise that we are filled with joy when we enter the presence of God (Psalm 16:11). There is a Christmas sermon here that I have not yet preached about finding joy in the manger and then seeing Christ everywhere else.

What I have realized is how joy overcame me in receiving you as a gift. To hold you was to feel as if I was in the presence of God. Your entrance into our lives was not an accomplishment on our end but a creative act of the Divine, whereby something wonderful was shared with us not because we deserved it but because there is a love underlying the world that surpasses our understanding.

Being your dad has surpassed any expectations I could have held because those hopes were vested in an idea, in an anticipation of what might be. Now that you are here in the flesh, an actual person with your beautiful smile and quirky personality, those abstract notions have become concrete. As C.S. Lewis put

---

[2] Julian of Norwich, *Revelations of Divine Love*, trans. Barry Windeatt (London: Oxford University Press, 2015).

it, "Joy itself, considered simply as an event in my own mind, turned out to be of no value at all. All the value lay in that of which Joy was the desiring."[3]

You have not only brought me joy. You *are* my joy. What an irony that I have written you this lengthy letter to say that in becoming your dad I have experienced a joy that cannot be put into words!

That reality has bolstered my faith. It is the reason I dare to call you a miracle. I look at you, behold God, and discover the fullness of joy anew.

With steadfast love,

Dad

---

[3] C.S. Lewis, *Surprised by Joy* (London: Geoffrey Bles, 1955).

Dear Sons,

Sometimes one does everything "by the book" and still one's efforts fail. One of my fondest memories growing up was gardening with my mom. Her gardens were always full of tomatoes, green beans, squash, and other delicious vegetables. The tomato vines were sometimes taller than me! Everything that I know about gardening I learned from my mother.

Likewise, my favorite thing to do with you has been gardening. You have helped me pick out seeds, plant them, water, harvest, cover them from frosts, and pull out everything before Old Man Winter makes his presence known for the season. I love to see your joy when I tell you that we can go outside to tend the garden. Some people are snobby about selecting wine. You have become snobby about eating store-bought tomatoes.

I try to teach you how to garden in the best ways, including with a careful eye on the weather in the spring to see when it is safe to plant delicate vegetables, especially in Colorado. We usually wait until Mother's Day weekend, which is the advice of many local gardeners. One year, I checked the weather to confirm that for the next ten days the temperature was not supposed to drop below 45 degrees Fahrenheit. With that good news, we planted! As usual, you gardened in your pajamas.

Eight days after we finished planting, I uncovered the garden because the temperatures were rising and rain was forthcoming to help the plants grow. Yet over the course of the day, the weather forecast changed. I had a meeting at church that night. During the meeting, we noticed that it had begun to snow. That surprised everyone because snow had not been in the forecast. None of the roads had been prepared for snow. I almost had to walk home because of the number of car wrecks on the road. I ended up making it home by taking a number of side streets. To top it off, I got stuck in the driveway, but I got home.

My first act (alone, since you were asleep in bed) was to try to salvage the exposed plants. We ended up losing about a third of our garden, but all things considered this felt like a victory. When you woke up, still in your pajamas, I held you in my arms and showed you the garden through the windows of our living room. I said, "Sons, sometimes, you do everything right and things still do not work out." You said that it was OK because we could always just plant more vegetables. You offered to help me go to the store and do the necessary work in the garden.

You taught me one of the joys of being dad on that day; gardeners can always replant. When something goes wrong in life, people often become fatalistic and begin to believe that success is no longer possible. That rigidness gets in the way of creativity and grace. I thought that we were simply planting a garden, but you, intentionally or not, were teaching me a lesson on grace.

Gardening is all about doing your best while knowing that there are a variety of things that can mess it up, most of them beyond your control. Yes, I have been planting the garden with you, but unknowingly at times I have also been planting more important things that will nurture our relationship forever.

One of the first songs that I listened to after I found out that you were making me a dad was "Watching You" by Rodney Adkins. It is a wonderful country song about the trouble and joy that comes when someone watches you and "wants to do everything that you do." The dad in the story realizes that his son does some of the same unfortunate things that he does. Yet the boy also mimics some of dad's good habits gleaned through observation. As is often said, imitation is the sincerest form of flattery. Nonetheless, most dads do not want their boys to emulate them.

For me, the joy of fatherhood is watching you. I love watching you find a tomato in the garden or a little bunch of red currants hiding at the base of the bush. I love watching you find joy in something because, as the song goes, "I want to do everything that you do." One of your best gifts to me is sharing life with me.

I grew up in Huntsville, Alabama. Even though my parents did not work in the space industry there, I still fell in love with that world. It fascinates me. Recently, Jupiter and Saturn appeared as one bright star in the sky. The experience has a few names, including the "Christmas Star" or the "Star of Bethlehem." I ended my church meeting as soon as possible to take you outside to experience the moment. I showed you maps of the solar system with the planets to try to explain what was going on. Once outside, I told you that this had last happened about eight hundred years ago. I said that it would be sixty years until this occurred again. You giggled, then ran inside to tell Mom all about it. Clearly, you were going to get a telescope for your Christmas present.

Over the next few days, just before dinner, you said that you wanted to go and see Jupiter and Saturn again. Each time you asked how old you would be when it next happened. I told you again that you would be in your sixties! I wondered whether I would be alive the next time it happens. In 2080, I will be the ripe old age of ninety-seven. I imagine you visiting me in my retirement. Regardless of whether I am still alive then or not, I hope that you will take my great-grandchildren outside to look at the sky in wonder.

* * *

Now I'm going to go back a few years, before you were even born...

Sons, when Mom asked if we could have a conversation about trying to have children, my initial reaction left much to be desired. We were at a beer garden. I wish that I could blame my response on the alcohol, but more truthfully I responded as I did because it was not an easy time in my life. I was struggling with depression at that time due to my ministry context. I was full of self-doubt because I was unable to be the savior of a church on life support. Accusations and resentment met my efforts to lead change. Therefore, while Mom was ready to embark on parenthood, I thought I was too much of a failure to do so. I have a failure narrative in my life. When I shared this experience with a close friend, he told me that my fear of being a bad father would help me be a wonderful one. Still, the thought of someone calling me "Dada" scared me. I was terrified that you would watch me and pick up all of my bad habits.

I knew that you would have some of my genes and, likely, a lot of the same struggles with self-doubt. That I found terrifying! I did not want to pass that on to anyone. Selfishly, I did not want to relive that pain. In reality, being your father has brought out the best parts of who God made me to be.

You see pictures of me doing triathlon and obstacle course races and you want to do them too. We transformed our backyard into our own obstacle course. You want me to compete alongside you so we can share the same experience and you can follow my lead. You usually hesitate the first time at an obstacle until you see me do it. Then you complete the obstacle with no problem! I cannot wait to do races with you in the future!

In the Gospel of John, Jesus says that his followers will do "even greater things" than he did. Said alternatively, we will outdo Jesus! How daunting to do more than Jesus! These words from Jesus come in midst of his conversation about his impending death. Jesus insists that all that he has done will not end with his death. Instead, the amazing things that the Jesus community was doing will continue and even expand into today.

In life, it is easy to think that one will "have arrived" or "be good enough" when one can match what someone else has done. Jesus rejoices at the expectation that we will go above and beyond what he has done. In that same vein, I love seeing you reach your goals and look forward to seeing you outdo me!

Sons, in the Christian tradition there is an idea that sin is inescapably passed on to each generation. I have struggled with the notion of original sin for many years. It does not make sense biologically nor, more importantly, scripturally. I understand the Bible as saying that God calls everything created "good." The notion of original blessing fits better with my experience of God than does original sin. We are blessed and given the chance to be our good selves, as God declares in Genesis 1.

I want you to know that I will strive to pass on blessings to you rather than sins. I want you to know where your food comes from. I want you to know the joy of dirt underneath your fingernails as you eat a tomato straight off the vine, a tomato that you grew from seed. I hope that you will look up at the stars with wonder and amazement. When you experience the richness of creation, I want you to experience that original blessing—that original goodness—of God.

Your mother and I spent many days imagining what it would be like as your parents. I shared that I was eager to go hiking with you. I imagined you on my back in a hiking backpack. I had seen fathers doing that and I wanted to experience it. So we tried it. Both of us got over it quickly. You wanted to get off my back and walk on your own!

Both of you hike well for kids your size. As expected, you get tired quickly and then request to jump on the "Dada Express" down the mountain. Still, I am glad that when you hike, you want to walk on your own two feet instead of riding on my bike. We move slower when you hike because of the size of your stride and because you tend to stop to look at lots of things along the way. But that's a good thing! You have taught me to slow down when I move through life, including on the hiking trail. You have a way of squatting down to see worms, bugs, and rocks that invites me to stop as well. In other words, I am learning a lesson of which I need to be reminded frequently—that life is more about the journey than the destination.

The joy of fatherhood is not that I get to do things *for* you but *with* you. I know that I will have difficulty deciphering whether to do something for you, help you do it, or be nearby if you request help.

I can already tell that you usually want me to do things *with* you, not *for* you. However, sons, I want you to know that I am always willing to help when you get tired. The "Dada Express" will always be in operation for you, whether you are a toddler or a grown adult!

I recall being twenty-one and telling my parents that I wanted to study abroad in college. It was a big conversation in my family. It even involved my sister because she acted as a mediator. I was asking for support, not permission. I thought that I had come of age and had the right to make this decision. Eventually, my parents gave me permission/their blessing. Next, I told them that I did not want a cozy experience. I wanted to go to a place significantly different from the USA—Morocco. It is a predominantly Muslim country with a king. While I was there, I could experience Ramadan, the United States' presidential election from a different context, and much more. Again, the question about permission or blessing arose. I know that this situation was difficult for them. I recall leaving a note for my mom about putting faith in God because it seemed particularly difficult for her to see her baby go across the ocean for a semester. She later realized that I am similar to her mother who likewise loved to experience the world. She did not mean it as a compliment, but that is how I took it.

I know that I will have this same pain with you. I might reluctantly give you my permission/blessing to do something, but please know that I am glad to see you walk on your own two feet. If needed, I will always get my hiking backpack and come and get you—wherever in the world you are.

The joy of fatherhood is that I get to be like the side of a pool. You hold on to me for a long time while in the water. One day, you will push off really hard and it will hurt me more than you. You will swim until you get tired and then come back to me to rest. Then, you will push off again and come back. Sons, please know that I will find joy being kicked all the time like the side of a pool because I know that it is the only way to do fatherhood.

I know that you will never learn how to swim for yourselves if you only hold on to me. I want you to push off and swim. I will be here when you need me. When I am gone, I hope to have equipped you well enough not to need those adorable "arm floaties" or to hold on to the side of the pool.

I realize that I will try to do everything by the book as a perfectionist. Yet, as with gardening, not everything will be perfect. That is to be expected. I hope that you will be in your pajamas when it happens—just as you were when part of the garden was destroyed—because tomorrow is a new day no matter what happened today. It is in this spirit that the risen Christ greeted his disciples (who seemed to have failed over and over) by offering them breakfast on the beach.

Just as Jesus never gave up on Peter, I will never give up on you.

My dream for you is that you will always try to replant when the storms of life come. When you see others feeling daunted by an obstacle, I pray that you will show them how to get over it. I hope that you will find joy in fatherhood too. It's the best! Fair warning: I will be watching you. I will watch as your children try to emulate you, as you do me!

With seeds in my hand,

Dad

Notes for My Letter about the Joy of Fatherhood

2

The Pressures That Young Men Face

Dear Sons,

As a young man, I was often told that I was too sensitive. Most summers, I volunteered to be a keynote speaker or chaplain at the annual one-week church camp with either middle or high school students. While there, I led a variety of interest groups around sports because I love to be active. However, I was also always eager to lead an interest group around the practice of a Clearness Committee.

A Clearness Committee is a beautiful Quaker (or Religious Society of Friends) practice that can be summed up as a trusted group of individuals surrounding you with questions to help you find your inner light or true direction as you wrestle with a question or topic. In my experience, such summer camps groups are usually predominantly young women, with a few brave boys.

In 2018, a young man shared with our group that he was worried about getting into a particular college. He painted a picture of a domino effect. He believed that if he did not get into his dream college, then everything else down the line would fail. Trusted individuals asked him curious questions. In doing so, we learned that he was only getting five hours of sleep per night. To get perfect grades to go along with a stellar list of extracurricular activities, he didn't feel he could sleep more than that. He shared that he was always stressed, exhausted, and overwhelmed. He admitted to feeling pressured to get into his dream college, believing that if he did not nobody would want to marry him. He anticipated all of the dominos of his neatly aligned life falling if he was not perfect in each moment. All of these layers showed that he was miserable. He had even contemplated suicide because he never thought that he could reach the imaginary finish line that his parents had painted for his life.

If you search my dresser drawers and office desk, you will find that I keep many of the notes that I receive from youth at church camp. I cherish them because they are words of encouragement that I need during times of stress and exhaustion. My stash includes a note from this young man. He said he was glad that he had not played football during "interest groups" on that day, and had gone instead to the Clearness Committee to seek clarity on how to handle a situation. Too often young men would rather chase a ball than talk about their feelings.

Sons, may you not chase a ball all the time, but instead be willing to discuss your emotions with a trusted group of individuals who can surround you with helpful questions.

In a recent survey by Plan International[4], an independent development and humanitarian organization which works in seventy-one countries across the world to advance children's rights and equality for girls, only 2 percent of male respondents from the ages of ten to nineteen said that the traits which society most values in boys are honesty and morality. In my experience, the definition of masculinity seems to become more narrowly defined each day. In the face of that, I promise to teach you, my sons, honesty and morality. I also promise to teach you to share your emotions with others. You cannot simply play sports and chase a ball around. Doing so is, literally, killing us.

[4] Tresa Undem and Ann Wang, *The State of Gender Equality for U.S. Adolescents* (Warwick, RI: Plan International USA, 2018)

It became clear to me early on that I would never be the biggest or fastest athlete, or a leader in any other metric when it came to sports. However, in the words of a pastor from my youth, I "always tried the hardest, which is good for something." Growing up in Alabama, there must have been a "bless your heart" before those words. I learned that in order to be successful, I had to be willing to keep trying harder than anyone else. I suppose that this is the moment to remind you that I passed on some of my genes to you. Therefore, you might have this experience with sports too.

* * *

Many young men say that there is just one narrow route to being successful. We have to "suck it up," "be a man," act combative, and dominate others, including women.

Sons, you never need to suck it up. May you tell others when it sucks.

Sons, you are truly a man when you share what words fail to fully articulate.

Sons, you will be most blessed when you are a peacemaker, according to Jesus.

Sons, may you never seek to dominate others as love should always be the path to deeper relationships with family, friends, and strangers.

* * *

If I ever sit on a Clearness Committee with you, I will ask you to share what might happen if you do not meet someone else's expectations. The young man whom I mentioned earlier thought that if he did not do something perfectly today, tomorrow would not turn out well and the future would be bleak. Sons, if like him you decide to change career trajectories, I will be glad that you remained open to new possibilities. My love is never seasonal or dependent upon any imaginary goal you think you need to attain in order to be perceived as a success.

The only pressure that you will face from me is to be honest and moral. The former means always speaking the truth, including to yourself. The latter means being aware of how your actions affect others. I believe that honesty and morality are the most fruitful ways to bring about an abundant life for you and those around you.

As you will learn, for thirty-five years I struggled with low self-worth and self-esteem. It was an up-and-down journey. I had voices in my head that seemed to be especially loud when things were not perfect. Back then, I assigned those voices to other people, but now I know it was my own voice behind the megaphone.

I do not mean to sound as if I have overcome the obstacles of low self-worth and self-esteem. I have simply become better equipped at anticipating these voices and removing the batteries from the megaphone to quiet the voices.

I first realized that I had reached this point at church camp in 2018. During an evening vespers service, a small group had time for each person to write something on a rock that they were trying to let go. Then, we were going to release them. With a permanent marker in my hand, I wrote what I have been writing for decades on numerous rocks at such times: low self-worth and low self-esteem.

Words fail to convey fully what I felt, but it was as if a weight had been taken off my shoulders. I suddenly realized that those feelings were not things that belonged on my rock anymore. Of course, I had *many* other things to write instead, but those particular two were no longer on my rock. At the end of the service, I sat alone in the chapel, crying. I knew that, after thirty-five years, I had reached a new point in my life. Ironically, this is the age when someone becomes eligible to be president. Apparently —at least for me—there is something about this age that assumes one has overcome less mature character traits and is now qualified to be the most powerful person in the world. In reality, being comfortable in one's own skin is what makes one powerful.

I do not know what you will write with a marker on your rocks. I do not know what voices will have access to a megaphone in your soul. However, I will always be ready to be a rock for you, offer up a different voice behind the megaphone, and cry with you.

I shed tears all the time. I tend to view my tears as a reminder of my baptism, which can mean a myriad of things. For John the Baptist, it had a layer of crossing the Jordan River, as the Israelites did in the Hebrew Bible. It was a sense of coming home after a long journey. Moses helped to start the journey, but it was the next generation that got to experience what it was like to come home. I hope to help you on this journey of "coming home." I might not make it to the end with you, but I hope that you will learn what truly matters in life earlier than I did. This is one of my many goals as your father.

* * *

When you cry, your tears are the way home.

Sons, the only way to come home is to be willing to share your emotions. As you do, if you are anything like me, you will cry. And that is more than ok as it is the path.

* * *

On the other side of the Jordan without tears and emotions, you will find only a desert. That way of living can *never* bring about life, life abundant (John 10:10). It leads only to destruction. My hope and dream for you is that you will see your tears as a baptism on the way home.

One day, if you choose, I will baptize you. It is a day that I have already begun to sketch in my soul. Together, we will be standing in water. At least one of us will be crying. I will be "well pleased" because you were willing to get into the water to cross over to a more abundant life (Matthew 3:17). My hope is that you will wash clean of all forms of the toxic masculinity that is a driving force in our world.

To borrow imagery from Jesus in Matthew 7:13, the easy, wide gate in our world is being a man who caves to the pressure of toxic masculinity. This gate leads to destruction and many enter through it. These pressures were etched into statues in the ancient world and into the souls of men today. Sons, may you enter through the narrow gate. It may take you thirty-five years, but once you get there, you will see the fraud of the pressures that men face. You may find yourselves offering Clearness Committees to youth in hopes of making a difference as I did.

Sons, I keep the thank you letters from participants at past church camps because I need words of encouragement from time to time. I have kept other cards and letters for that same reason. I need to surround myself with cheerleaders due to my inclination to be negative towards myself over the years.

In 2019, I completed my first Ironman event. It had been a goal of mine since high school. Years ago, on an extended layover at the Denver International Airport, I bought an Ironman hat at an airport kiosk as a way to mark my determination. Since that time, I have competed in numerous triathlons. My favorite part about triathlons is that nobody can be the best at every part of the race because swimmers are built differently than bikers. Bikers' legs are different from those who excel at running. In other words, the race reminds me of my humanity since I cannot win each segment of the race.

On the day of my thirty-sixth birthday, I dropped off my bike and participated in the Ironman race orientation. The race director reminded us all that everyone had to complete the swim by a certain time—or be disqualified. The race marshals would come to your rescue, but if you had taken too long, you would not be allowed to compete in the other segments of the race. Those following you via the Ironman app would be able to see that you were a DNF (did not finish). I sat there on the side of the lake next to mom, your brother, and you, silently wondering if I could make the cutoff. On race day, I did my personal best in swimming and biking. I was emotional throughout those segments because I had been dreaming about this day for decades. Finally, I put on my shoes and prepared to run to the finish line.

All went according to plan until miles four and five. The temperature that day was in the midnineties and I was nauseous, cramping, wishing that I had brought my asthma inhaler, and overheating in the dry heat of Boulder, Colorado (less than fifty miles from the airport where I bought my hat years before). Those aforementioned negative voices behind the megaphone were loud, really loud. Someone had given them the batteries that I had taken away.

My fear was that I would be labeled a DNF. I found myself asking difficult questions with miles ahead of me. Could I make it? Why had I wasted so much time and money only to fail? What would my friends and family say if I was a DNF?

Thankfully, I found a whole new part of me at that moment. I took the megaphone from those voices. They did not deserve residence in my soul. I gave the megaphone to better voices that deserve to reside in my soul: God, family (including your pep talk the day before the race), and friends. They told me that I could keep going. They said that I was already good enough. They said that they believed in me.

After that, I picked up speed with each mile. By the last few miles, I was sprinting! I ran my personal best mile that day. I ran with haste to a better way of being me, with the megaphone dragging behind me. When I heard the announcer call my name as I crossed the finish line, it was as if God was calling me home.

Inches past the finish line, I cried because I was overwhelmed with emotion. I shared this experience with the wife of a friend who helped me train for this race. She said that she loved to meet her spouse at the finish line because he always fell into her arms and cried like a baby. It is the only time that he showed that emotion and she loved it.

Sons, you are not the only one doing this race. All men are doing it. All of us have areas of life to which we are more suited than others. My prayer is that you will always be honest, moral, and willing to try, even decades later than expected. We need to throw ourselves into life and surrender the results. Notice I did not say "surrender *to* the results." Said alternatively, try your best and celebrate your effort, and don't compare yourself to others who are on the same journey.

The author of the letter to the Hebrews paints a picture of running a race with crowds watching (Hebrews 12). For some of us, the crowd is full of negative voices that say that we should give up. They might say that we are not good enough. They might call us failures. The author of this letter paints an image of "a great cloud of witnesses" *cheering for* us. We need to give them and not the negative voices the megaphone. If you will let me, my lips will always be on the other side of the megaphone urging you onward. Sons, when you cross each finish line, you can come home—into my arms.

With tears rolling down my face for you,

Dad

Dear Son,

I struggled to fit in as a kid. That meant I stood out.

During my preteen and early teenage years I wore a White Sox shirt to school every single day. I had dozens of different White Sox shirts in my closet. Jerseys, throwback logos, and even a purple T-shirt awaited me each morning ready to be worn as a form of self-expression.

This loyal devotion to my favorite baseball team emblazoned on my daily attire did not make me the most popular kid at school. I was not disliked, but I was different. I was an oddball.

I am sure a child psychologist could easily explain my behavior in expert terms. I am comfortable reducing my weird obsession to the cultivation of a unique identity.

I enjoyed success in school, but others were smarter than me. The theater crowd and the band kids were not my group. While I played sports, I was never the star athlete (or even all that well coordinated). But nobody was as fervent a White Sox fan as me. Those shirts made a statement. They were my way of nonconforming. They forced others to see me as an individual.

My particular way of doing this was perhaps strange, but each of us pursues this project in our own way. We all need to define ourselves. Maturing as a human being in modern Western society involves establishing an identity of one's own.

I came to appreciate this more fully while taking a class in divinity school. My pastoral care professor assigned a book called *The Stories We Live By* written by a psychologist named Dan McAdams. His basic argument is that individuals develop narratives about who they are. These accounts provide a sense of ourselves that allows us to function in the world.

One helpful summation of his work claims that:

> McAdams describes narrative identity as an internalized story you create about yourself — your own personal myth. Like myths, our narrative identity contains heroes and villains that help us or hold us back, major events that determine the plot, challenges overcome and suffering we have endured. When we want people to understand us, we share our story or parts of it with them."[5]

Psychological growth involves filling out this story. Beginning in childhood and running into our adult years, we are writing and refining this personal script. Some challenges defeat us. Others we overcome. We welcome supportive people into our lives who steer us towards opportunities. Alternatively, others prove obstacles to our goals, perhaps even acting maliciously towards us.

The trick is to tell a story that is genuinely yours rather than one determined by social conventions and the expectations of others. At one point, I grew tired of wearing White Sox shirts. I do not remember if something specifically provoked this or if being different just wore me out. Changing this pattern required a new wardrobe.

I disclosed my intentions on a shopping trip with my parents. We went to various stores with little luck. There was nothing that was obviously "me" (besides baseball shirts). Rather than taking some time to figure this out, I did the easy thing. We bought the same clothes every other kid was wearing. Upon returning to school, I now blended into the crowd but I felt uncomfortable in my own skin. The White Sox attire quickly returned.

In 1 Corinthians 13:11, the Apostle Paul famously says, "When I was a child, I talked like a child, I thought like a child,

---

[5] Emily Esfahan Smith, "The two kinds of stories we tell about ourselves," *IDEAS. TED.COM*, Jan. 12, 2017, https://ideas.ted.com/the-two-kinds-of-stories-we-tell-about-ourselves/.

I reasoned like a child. When I became a man, I put the ways of childhood behind me."

He was not talking about my clothing choices but about maturity in faith. Truly becoming a follower of Jesus requires growing up spiritually. It involves taking the biblical story and making it your own, of seeking after God not because you are supposed to but because there is nothing else you would rather do.

This shift from acting out of real desire instead of conforming to expectations is one of the most difficult traits to master. In a quite morbid quote, the sixteenth-century French writer Francois de La Rochefoucauld wrote, "few people are well-acquainted with death. It is generally submitted to through stupor and custom, not resolution: most [people] die merely because they cannot help it."[6]

His point about living and dying is that few people bother to think deeply about how they live. Most people follow the crowd. They take their cues from others rather than daring to determine for themselves how they will spend their days.

When I was in high school, I wanted to be really into physical fitness. All my friends were hitting the weight room so they could hit a baseball harder, run across the football field faster, and—let's be honest—impress girls.

I convinced my parents to buy some weight equipment for our basement. Feeling insecure about my lack of experience in the gym, I preferred to work out in the privacy of our home. Of course, what really happened is that the equipment went unused. There was no discipline or accountability on my part. Simply having the weightlifting machines did not help my physical fitness at all.

Once we learned that you were on the way, I recommitted myself to getting physically healthy. I wanted to ensure my own

---

[6] Quoted in Geoffrey Scarre, *Death* (Montreal: McGill-Queen's University Press, 2007).

stamina would keep up with your anticipated energy. Even more, I worried about not being around to see you grow up. My health was not poor but it was not remarkable either.

So, I went to the gym. I started lifting weights. I tried running again. It was painful.

The amount on my barbell looked pretty puny compared to the next guy. I was breathing harder than people twice my age who had run three times as far.

But that did not matter anymore. My objective was not to look good for others. I was driven by a personal goal that made everything else irrelevant. My thinking about physical fitness had matured. In this particular area, I was no longer a child.

What is interesting in Paul's admonition is that he's not being disparaging towards children. Kids should be expected to act like kids. The problem arises when adults refuse to grow up. You cannot fault a child for acting their age.

I learned this firsthand when talking with teenagers in a church youth group. Every Wednesday they would show up at church bringing with them all sorts of gossip, drama, and hurt. It was clear they considered all of this to be significant. The snide comment by a friend or a relationship ending abruptly cut deeply.

They lacked perspective. It was impossible for them to see that their girlfriend probably was not the love of their life when their lack of experience made them seem like soulmates. They presumed that the disappointment or embarrassment they were feeling in that moment was life-changing and life-defining.

In reality, none of it really matters. A lot of what happens in our teenage years signifies very little. There are obvious exceptions for the truly big stuff: a loved one dying, becoming addicted to something, discovering one's orientation or identity. None of these conversations were about anything approaching that level of importance.

This is exactly how teenagers are wired to behave. No amount of wisdom from me could change their minds because biology exerts a powerful force.

As Dan Siegel, an expert on adolescent brain development, puts it, "Why would it be natural to turn toward your peers as an adolescent? Because that's on whom you're going to depend on when you leave home." He adds:

> One really big downside is that membership with an adolescent peer group—even if it's just one other person—can feel like a matter of life and death: 'If I don't have at least one peer that I'm connected with, I'm gonna die.' That's what millions and millions of years of evolution are telling this adolescent. So if there's a party going on, the teen may very well feel as though she's going to die if she doesn't go.[7]

Wanting the affirmation of peers during our adolescent years is instinctual. Knowing that others are key to our survival, evolution hardwires our brains to seek out approval and connection. All of us are social creatures by nature. Belonging to a group is about more than caving in to peer pressure. It reflects the human need for community in order to thrive over the course of our lives.

This puts us both in a conundrum.

On your end, you must thread a difficult needle. You have a story to write that must be your own. Nobody else is like you. Nobody else is made up of the same thoughts and feelings, nor will anyone have exactly the same experiences or set of responses. The life that unfolds will be uniquely yours.

This is true for everybody but few bother to ponder its implications. Handed a distinct set of ingredients, most people tend

---

[7] Daniel Siegel, "How the Teen Brain Transforms Relationships, *Greater Good Magazine,* August 12, 2014, https://greatergood.berkeley.edu/article/item/how_the_teen_brain_transforms_relationships.

to cook a rather unconventional meal. Instead of mastering the cuisine they most enjoy, one closely reflecting their preferences and personality, they produce what is easiest or expected.

You have the opportunity to take the ingredients of your life and cook a gourmet meal determined by your own tastes. Yet you will want others to like your cooking. You want your dinner table to be full of people eager to dine with you and who relish the opportunity to eat what you prepare.

Those whose approval you seek will give you advice. They will foist their wishes upon you and ask you to embrace their ideas. You will feel pressure to follow their lead, and we need to be honest, there will be times when you pressure others in the same way. At times they will lead you into wonderful new discoveries. At other points, they may lead you astray in ways that force you to retrace your steps or worse.

Your job is to sort this all out. Discernment involves judging well. That is your task. You must evaluate all the influences and pressures alongside your own wishes and determine how it all fits together within your story.

My problem is figuring out what role to play. Ideally, I would be the wise guide as you mature, steering you adroitly through the sometimes turbulent waters until you reach the point of putting away childish things. Drawing on my own experiences, I would be a valuable sounding board in your discernment by providing the perspective you need but the passage of time does not yet allow you to have.

I fear falling short of that ideal. I fear not being able to see beyond my own limitations in ways that doom you to repeat my mistakes. Instead of helping you withstand the pressures of life, I fear becoming one more person adding to them. Recognizing that, if this becomes true, the pressures I add to you are likely to be greater than others.

This letter is meant to serve two purposes. First, I hope it encourages you to chart your own course. Even at an early age,

I see so much in you that is worth cultivating. I want you to find forms of self-expression that lead to your flourishing. Second, these words give you permission to hold me accountable, to tell me when I cross the line from advocate to zealot and to demand I take a step back.

I also do not want to scare you. The pressures of childhood are often uncomfortable, but they have their own formative value. There's a reason these years are referred to as "formative." You will learn a tremendous amount about yourself, the world around you, and others within it. These experiences will change you in profound ways.

Diamonds serve as a wonderful analogy. Counted among the most beautiful objects in the world, they originate deep beneath the Earth's surface. "Obviously in that part of the Earth it's very hot," explains Jeffrey Post of the Smithsonian National Museum of Natural History. "There's a lot of pressure, the weight of the overlying rock bearing down, so that combination of high temperature and high pressure is what's necessary to grow diamond crystals in the Earth."[8]

Beholding the beauty of a diamond is only possible because of these extreme conditions. The heat and pressure are integral in forming the jewel that causes us to marvel. I would like to believe the same is true about the pressures and challenges we face in life. They form and refine us into more beautiful creatures.

The Apostle Paul appears to think along similar lines when he writes in 2 Corinthians that:

> We are hard pressed on every side, but not crushed; perplexed, but not in despair; persecuted, but not abandoned; struck down, but not destroyed. We always carry around in our body the death of Jesus, so that the life of

---

[8] Cate Lineberry, "Diamonds Unearthed," *Smithsonian Magazine*, December 2006, https://www.smithsonianmag.com/science-nature/diamonds-unearthed-141629226/.

Jesus may also be revealed in our body. For we who are alive are always being given over to death for Jesus' sake, so that his life may also be revealed in our mortal body. So then, death is at work in us, but life is at work in you. (4:8–12 NIV)

As we write the stories of our lives, they will include chapters about the pressures we faced and, hopefully, the ways we responded to them that witness to the beautiful life God reveals in Jesus Christ.

With love,

Dad

Notes for My Letter about the Pressures that Young Men Face

3

Helping to Break the Glass Ceiling

Dear Son,

I still get a chuckle recalling the scene. You are standing on the changing table frustrated and shouting, "there's no Skye!" The target of your ire was a new pair of Paw Patrol pajamas featuring several of the pups from the TV show but not your favorite one, who also happens to be one of only two female characters. Her exclusion was unacceptable to you, and the world (or at least everyone in our house) was going to hear about it.

While inclusivity may not have motivated your protests that night, I hope it portends a lifelong commitment to advocating for gender equity. Too many men have invested their energies opposing such equality and instead promoting the subjugation of women. This must stop. You, son, have the opportunity to be a different kind of man with regards to the way our society chooses to include or exclude women.

Unfortunately, the refusal to see men and women as equals is an intense problem within American Christianity. This is because too many church structures are designed to support and preserve a patriarchal order, where men wield power and exert control. We even read the Bible through this lens, resulting in a twisted view of gender roles called "complementarianism" that inhibits our flourishing. Beth Allison Bar, a historian at Baylor University, describes it as the idea that:

> Women and men have divinely ordained, distinct gender roles that are not interchangeable. Women are divinely ordained to follow male headship and to be primarily focused on domestic tasks: family and home. Men are divinely ordained to lead and not just in the church and in the family, but it also spills over into the outside — the cultural world, the economic world.[9]

When I was a teenager, just beginning to take my own faith seriously, a friend tried to convince me that women could not be leaders in the church. Their role was to be subservient to men. This friend then impressively reeled off a bunch of Bible verses —a practice I later learned was called proof texting because of the way it uses scripture out of context as proof— in support of this argument for Christian patriarchy.

Newly confused, I posed the question to my grandfather (that would be great-grandpa to you), who is one of the wisest Christians I know. Having seen him serve alongside women elders and guided by female board chairs, I presumed he would have a rebuttal to my friend. Grandpa did not disappoint. "Have you ever seen a church operate without women in leadership?" he asked me rhetorically. "*Some* churches appropriately honor the contributions of women but *all* churches depend upon them."

I came to learn that the scriptural passages being cited by those wanting to limit women in church leadership were quite selective. Like a cynical politician who ignores inconvenient facts in order to ram through an agenda, this particular breed of Christian had motives other than fidelity to God's Word.

---

[9] Emily McFarlan Miller, "Beth Allison Barr wants Christians to know where 'biblical womanhood' comes from (it's not the Bible)," *Religion News Service,* April 20, 2021, https://religionnews.com/2021/04/20/beth-allison-barr-wants-christians-to-know-where-biblical-womanhood-comes-from-and-its-not-the-bible/.

Such Christians failed to mention the passage in Romans where the Apostle Paul references working alongside Phoebe and Priscilla to advance the sharing of the Gospel. Nor did such Christians talk about the women who found Jesus' tomb empty and became the first ones to preach his resurrection. While the events of the Bible occurred within sociohistorical contexts that often reflected views towards women that we no longer embrace, there are many prominent women within scripture and many episodes throughout the Bible in which women play a leading role that reveals their participation in the unfolding ways of God. Those denying this fact are pursuing their own narrow-minded purposes.

Even as the church makes great strides on issues of gender equity relative to past eras, the progress proves halting at times. Sociologists describe a "stained glass ceiling" which blocks female ministers from serving in prominent pulpits or positions. Instead, they are relegated to smaller, struggling congregations and to associate positions that unfairly restrict career paths. Even the denominations that formally grant women the same status as men still struggle to realize the equality they profess. It is shocking to imagine the costs of this sin in terms of the leadership our churches miss out on and the wounds inflicted by humans on those whom God has called to serve.

To male pastors, this issue can seem rather abstract. We do not experience it directly. This can make us quick to downplay or dismiss such reports as problems that exist in other places but not around us. In fact the discrimination is far closer than we realize. It is no exaggeration to tell you that in every church where I have worshiped or pastored for any length of time this issue has reared its ugly head. "I am not sure our church is ready for a woman pastor," an elder once quipped. In a different location, a matriarch of the church sidled up to me and quietly whispered on Sunday when a guest (female) preacher was visiting, "I just struggle to listen when a woman is in the pulpit." From comments about the tone of their voice to their choice of clothing,

I have been shocked more than once about the disparaging remarks so easily uttered about women leaders by men within the body of Christ.

And if those comments were made to me, just imagine what women ministers feel and hear directly! Or, worse yet, what is said in the church parking lot or gossiped about beyond the ear of any minister.

I always pushed back (gently) when these moments arose. I would redirect the conversation by pointing out the pastor's talents or softly scold by saying, "Everyone has different gifts but they all deserve appreciation by the church."

My responses made me part of the problem.

Whether out of cowardice or awkwardness, I struggled and failed to find the force necessary to say, "This conversation is inappropriate and has to stop. There are too many double standards and unfair expectations placed on clergy who are women. The church's sinful history of male domination continues to fester even in a congregation as progressive as this one. I will not tolerate it a moment longer or perpetuate it any further."

Those words are easy to write in this letter. They are difficult to speak in a fraught encounter where they will likely cause offense. I regret my unintentional but real contributions to this injustice. I resolve to do better going forward. Time will undoubtedly provide a test for me to pass or fail.

Relatedly, the rise of ordained female ministers is occurring at a time of immense struggle for the institutional church. Caused by a complicated mix of internal scandals (financial mismanagement, sexual abuse, etc.) and external trends (the secularization of society, rise of Christian nationalism, and increased individualism), those women who do shatter the stained glass ceiling find the tasks before them more complicated than ones from the past. Researchers label this the "stained glass cliff," describing the phenomenon of women being promoted into top positions at times of crisis that increase the likelihood of failure. Finally allowed to reach the top on the basis of their talent, they find themselves stewarding imperiled churches and organizations.

While we must speak honestly about these realities, the injustices of the past cannot be changed and the structural challenges of the present cannot be avoided. All the women ordained into ministry now does not change those who were denied their calling before. Those wounds were not healed; their talents were not received.

As more women enter religious leadership, little can be done about the serious headwinds facing churches, denominations, and Christian institutions of all kinds. Many of these leaders will prove successful beyond imagination, but the paths they will have to traverse are made immensely more difficult by virtue of these forces. Others will encounter failures for which they will be undeservedly blamed because their faithful witness will be overwhelmed by what was beyond their control.

This is the moment where I am supposed to have something profound to say to you, to offer you a bit of wisdom you had not considered that resolves all the tension. Having outlined a weighty problem to a son, a father is then expected to provide a way to remove the burden. The only answer I can suggest falls short of that goal. It begins with lament.

Here is a profoundly biblical response to the pain caused by injustice. Instead of despairing that nothing will ever change, lament expresses sadness and anger at the current state of affairs but refuses to give in to the temptation of fatalism. What is happening right now is wrong. Yet perhaps our disturbing cries will be heard by God and others in a way that alters the future.

Lament is present throughout the Bible but especially in the Psalms and, of course, Lamentations. Despite the sacredness of this response, many American Christians reject it entirely or struggle to grasp its power. As Soong-Chan Rah, a theologian and biblical commentator, eloquently writes:

The American church avoids lament. Consequently the underlying narrative of suffering that requires lament is lost in lieu of a triumphalistic, victorious narrative. We forget the necessity of lament over suffering and pain. Absence doesn't make the heart grow fonder. Absence makes the heart forget. The absence of lament in the liturgy of the American church results in the loss of memory.[10]

To make any real progress on gender inequality within church and society, we cannot forget the transgressions of the past. Lament is the faithful response. We first must remember and grieve all that has gone wrong if there is any hope of getting things right.

Lament is a necessary step, but it is not the final one. For after we have expressed our anguish, we must then undertake the work of repentance. If Christianity is stereotyped by some as superficial, the concept of repentance corrects that misunderstanding. Repentance involves recognizing an error, expressing contrition for it, and then committing to a different way of living that avoids repeating the sin. As the New Testament scholar Matt Skinner puts it, repentance "refers to a changed mind, to a new way of seeing things, to being persuaded to adopt a different perspective."[11] This idea is not just about admitting a mistake and apologizing. It is hard work.

I regularly preach that being repentant means recognizing your own perspective is too limited and inevitably wrong, confessing the sins caused by that narrowness, and then enlarging one's worldview so that we see the world and others as God

---

[10] Soong-Chan Rah, "The American Church's Absence of Lament," *Sojourners*, October 24, 2013, https://sojo.net/articles/12-years-slave/american-churchs-absence-lament.

[11] Mat Skinner, "Commentary on Luke 13:1-9," *Working Preacher*, March 7, 2010, https://www.workingpreacher.org/commentaries/revised-common-lectionary/third-sunday-in-lent-3/commentary-on-luke-131-9.

intends. This is Jesus' exhortation to his followers to "Repent!" because the reign of God is close at hand (Matthew 4:17).

When it comes to equality between men and women, in church and society, lament and repentance are both in order. Much of our past is ugly and that cannot be ignored. Having named the failures, we become responsible for creating a future that is radically different because our outrage at the errors from before motivate us to reimagine and reorder our relationships in ways that are more just. We seek closer accord with the equal status that all of us have before God.

There is no way to deny the complicity of the institutional church in promoting an unequal society, but glimmers of hope are emerging that even some of the most reluctant actors are embracing repentance. Saddleback Church, led for decades by Rick Warren, might be the best known church in America today. With tens of thousands of members and operating on a global stage, anything it does has far-reaching ripple effects.

So, the church drew a lot of attention in May of 2021 when it ordained three female pastors. As a congregation within the Southern Baptist Convention (SBC), Saddleback's provocative act defied both its own history and the current strictures of the denomination. The ensuing debate featured patriarchal defenses of the SBC's prohibition on women's ordination and newfound hope that momentum for change was building within America's largest Protestant denomination.

One advocate for women's ordination, Ashley Easter, put the moment in perspective by tweeting out, "I'm glad Saddleback Church ordained 3 of their first women pastors. But don't forget these women have been with the church since the 90s. That's how long it takes for a church to say 'oh, these women are pastoral.' Thats [sic] the hill women have to climb."[12]

---

[12] Ashley Easter (@ashleymeaster), Twitter, May 8, 2012, 4:06 pm, https://twitter.com/ashleymeaster/status/1391137353415135233.

Her tweet contains an implicit question for you and me, my sons: Are we making that hill more or less steep? As men who benefit from the privileges that come with living in a patriarchal society, are we using our power to undermine or sustain the present inequalities of the system?

My son, I pray that your early outrage at Skye's exclusion from the picture on your Paw Patrol pajamas never subsides. As the years ahead unfold, I hope you will meet every moment of gender inequality you witness with equal indignation. In doing so, you can become part of the collective repentance both church and society need to practice.

With love,

Dad

Dear Sons,

One third of women today experience sexual or physical abuse, according to the World Health Organization. When I married your mom, she was the legal guardian for her younger brothers due to the death of her mother. She, her brothers, and her male cat moved into my tiny condo. Because your mom's mother was a single mother, mom's younger brothers had never lived with a man besides a brief transitional housing situation. I told her brothers that my number one goal was showing them a way of being a good man. I feel that weight even more so with you because people see you as smaller versions of me.

I was blessed to have positive role models in this way. Your grandmother would say to me, "Just be a good man like your dad." I remember watching him and how he interacted with others, especially women. I know other boys did not have a father who was as good as mine. I am trying to provide you with the same example he offered to me.

I have learned in life that God's image dwells equally in all people. Yet, that universal reality is not recognized by many others. I was blessed to be raised in a church with leadership that represented God's image. I did not question women being in church leadership because I have been used to it my entire life.

One of the ways in which men keep women from breaking the glass ceiling is through abuse or (verbal, emotional, or physical) violence. One of my favorite games growing up was Mike Tyson's Punch-Out!! boxing game on the original Nintendo. When I was mad growing up, I would play this game. One of the opponents happened to look just like your grandfather. All of the opponents were much bigger than the character who I was playing—a white guy in a muscle shirt with dark hair. My heart aches as I think about it now because I thought that I could resolve situations with violence. Without knowing it at the time, I identified with the small white guy who could finally be heard thanks to violence.

Some of the strongest people I know are women, including your mother. Yet, in our world, strong women are often ridiculed. According to some people's social construction of what it means to be a woman, they should not be strong, opinionated, or have high aspirations. One of the most common understandings of women in the world is that they are meant to be dominated—specifically to be dominated by men. Let me tell you: Men do not have to dominate others in order to make a difference.

Your great-grandfather served in the Navy in World War II. He wrote to his commanding officers about the behavior of his fellow sailors when they got on dry land. They were acting in ways that were contrary to being a "good man," according to your great-grandfather. Of course, that letter got him put in charge of a commission to confront these types of behaviors in the Navy! He was able to make a difference without dominating others.

Sons, in many ways, we need to confront our fellow men when it comes to our problems. Too often, it is women confronting men about it. Obviously, this needs to be done, but we need to "deal with our own." Confronting toxic masculinity is a problem for *men*. Part of this effort needs to include the images of masculinity that form us.

In college, I was a part of a men's Bible study. We read a book written by a man about what it meant to be a godly man. I recall what reading that book and the conversations around it did to my relationship at the time. To sum it up, as the man, I was supposed to be the leader in the relationship. It did not go well. It was contrary to what our relationship had been up to that point and, honestly, to what I desired in a relationship. Later that year, a close friend of mine wrote in the school newspaper about her experience of assault while in a fraternity hall. She was ridiculed and publicly shamed. I wish I had done more back then to publicly voice my support of her. I failed at being a "good man" at that moment. Instead, I reserved being a "good man" behind the scenes with her instead of with other men (many of whom were in that aforementioned Bible study).

When I went back to school for my doctorate, I read a book that was written by two women who had experienced abuse. I recall what reading that book and the conversations around it did to my relationship with your mother. We had beautiful and eye-opening conversations about what it meant to be in a true, live-giving, and God-honoring relationship.

I still have the book from my doctoral studies. I no longer have the book that I read in college. I do not want to be formed by that understanding of what it means to be a man in a heterosexual relationship. The effort to break the glass ceiling is an important part of my role as your father. I feel the weight of that responsibility each time we interact as a family at home. I feel it when we go camping and you can easily watch my interactions with your mother. I feel it all the time, as I should.

Sons, the weight of responsibility to empower others is on men. Many people disagree with me. Most of those people are men. They are afraid that men are losing their perceived God-given positions in families and society. In reality, God has been seeking to empower all people who each fully reflect the image of God, but there are systems and institutions that are preventing it. Our family is different.

Sons, you come from a family where one side has fairly short men. Your great-grandmother was taller than her father-in-law. In World War I, your great-great grandfather was turned down by each branch of the military due to his height. At a recruiter's office, he was told that the person taking his measurements would look away for a bit. When they came back around, if he was tall enough, he would be able to enter the Army. Your great-great-grandfather stood on his tippy toes to be able to serve. It also helped that the height requirements changed as World War I dragged on. Years later, your great-grandfather lived a similar experience seeking to serve in World War II. We are a family whose men sometimes have to stand on their tippy toes to be able to serve.

Sons, you may feel insignificant at times. You may think that you cannot make a difference in the world. Trust me, you *will* make a difference. If you have to stand on your tippy toes in order to do so, all the better!

To make the world better reflect God's image, all men need to stand on their metaphorical tippy toes and become something better. At stake is not only over half of humanity, but our entire shared humanity. I do not know if I can fully define a "true man." However, I know that it involves acknowledging our privilege and striving for a world that better reflects God's image.

One of the many reasons why I support equal pay for women is that it gives women in abusive heterosexual relationships the financial means to exit that relationship. In other words, they are not dependent on a man for financial security. Further, in some faith traditions, a woman's security in the afterlife is dependent on a man. These understandings of gender put the weight of responsibility upon us men—"on earth as it is in heaven." With this responsibility, comes the need for us to say "I do not know" and be willing to learn from the experience of others.

Sons, when you were young, you often said that you knew the answer to things when you did not. Believe me, you never have to pretend you know all of the answers. One of my favorite sermons that I shared was entitled "The Smartest People Say 'I Do Not Know.'" I recall the next elders' meeting after I preached that sermon. The elders who were men voiced some concerns about the sermon. Meanwhile, the women who served as elders said that it spoke to their experience of life. It seems as if men feel the weight of having to know all of the answers.

In my experience, pretending to know all of the answers only creates disasters. Our family has already experienced this when I got our family lost on a hike (or two). I realize that I should have said "I do not know where we are."

I used to scoff at the idea that there were not always clear answers to questions. At that time in my life, many things seemed very clear— "black and white." I was so wrong! In my experience, life is the opposite to one of the lines in "Amazing Grace." The lyrics are "I once was blind, but now I see." For me, what makes grace truly amazing is that I once thought I could see, but I was truly blind. Said differently, it may have taken a while, but I am becoming more aware of my previous blind spots. This is what it means to not have all of the answers.

I have been around men who knew that they were wrong, but could not admit it. They felt they had to maintain the facade. It destroyed them. Most of the women that I know are willing to live in the beautiful rainbow between the black and white world that some create. There is great wisdom in those moments. I have learned to ask better questions and go where they lead me. For many men, that is impossible.

I share these stories about our family and our faith tradition because they have formed us and will continue to form us. When you were being knit together in your mother's womb (Psalm 139), we thought about our pasts, but we also thought about our preferred future for you. Therefore, we were deliberate when we chose the names that you would carry.

Malachi, you carry the name of a Hebrew prophet who asked an astonishing twenty-two questions recorded in eighty-eight verses. They were hard, gut-wrenching questions that rarely had a clear answer. We chose that name because we dreamed that you would be a man who would be willing to wrestle with difficult questions, learn from others around you especially those who have been silenced, those with disabilities, those from the Global South, those who love someone of the same gender, and those who do not fit neatly into the socially constructed understanding of gender, etc.

Zion, you are named after the Hebrew word that means sanctuary or safe place of refuge. Our dream for you is that you will be a safe place of refuge for everything and everyone who bears the imprint of God. Our world needs men who publicly stand with women when they dare to report an assault. Our world needs men who will ensure that a sanctuary is made for all persons, especially those who have been and are being marginalized.

Sons, your great-grandfather always wanted a son. Instead, he got three daughters. My mother always talked about how she was more of a "tomboy." She ended up playing in the mud and fishing, which boys typically do more than girls. Yet my mother taught me everything that I learned about fishing. Growing up, I recall her regularly outfishing the men around her. She would relish the moment, even as her dad watched and still yearned for a son of his own.

Sons, when I taught you how to fish, I spoke constantly about my mother being the one who had taught me. As one grows older, one thinks about all that one passes on to others. Paul thought about it when he wrote to the church in Corinth and passed on what was shared with him. I continually think about all that I want to pass on to you. For me, one of the central pieces of what it means to be your father is showing you an example of what it means to be a good man.

Our efforts as men to ensure a better world are not simply because we have women in our lives such as grandmothers, mothers, sisters, daughters, aunts, nieces, etc. We work for a more just world for women and all who have been marginalized because that is what makes a good man. We do not need to break the glass ceiling for women; we need to remove it. I believe that it starts at home with how I raise you—by my actions and words.

Yet words have not always come easy to me. I did not have complete hearing until I was in high school. Because of that, I stuttered all the time. In fact, I still stutter at times. I know the difficult sounds for me. I try to place them in the middle of a sentence to help me gloss over them. However, even to this day, I stutter when I am not confident or when I am unsure about something. I struggle to push the air out of my mouth. I was able to overcome this struggle thanks, in large part, to my mother driving me to countless doctors' appointments for my ears.

Sons, there are many people in our world who struggle to be heard. It is not their fault. It is mostly the fault of men who install glass ceilings above the heads of women and other individuals who have been marginalized. I am so keen to teach you how to be a good man because I believe that a better future will require men who ask good questions and act as sanctuaries to all of God's beloved.

I wish that I could selectively give you things that I wish to pass on. One of the items at the top of that list is breaking the glass ceiling. Although I am afraid that you might inherit my self-doubt, low self-worth, and self-esteem issues, I hope that you will see the way in which I treat women around me as (to quote a beloved hymn) "equal partners in Christ's service, called to ministries of grace.[13]"

May you be the spark to get the fire going,

Dad

---

[13] "Called As Partner's in Christ's Service," by Jane Parker Huber and John Zundel [PD].

Notes for My Letter about Helping to Break the Glass Ceiling

4

Seeing Color in a World of Black and White

Dear Sons,

Sometimes, you sing a song in the shower when you are eight years old only to have it affect you when you are in your thirties. In 1991, Michael Jackson came out with his hit song entitled "Black or White." Jackson was accused of changing his skin color through cosmetic procedures. He was tired of the racism that he faced, which he called the devil in his hit song.

Racism is a sort of devil that destroys God's image in people. In Genesis 1, the author writes that everything was *tov*—good. Most people think that the word refers to an object that it is describing. However, it also refers to the ties between things. For God, it was good that all things existed and that all existence was connected. Since creation, it seems, God has been creating and honoring diversity. Sadly, many people misconstrue *tov* as something that relates to their specific tribe—political, economic, ethnic, etc.

Sons, my hope and prayer is that you will strive to promote the *tov* between all of God's creation. I need to warn you that you will not fit into the Black and white categories that works for some people. You are *tov*. You are biracial and being such is part of what makes you *tov*.

I want to tell you about St. Joseph's Mission School, which began as a mission to the Black community of my home town of Huntsville, Alabama, in the 1950s. The primary building was a former plantation home dating back to the Civil War. About a decade later, George Wallace, a fierce segregationist, became governor of Alabama. On June 11, 1963, he stood in front of the schoolhouse door at the University of Alabama to prevent two Black students from enrolling. He was fulfilling a campaign promise: "Segregation now, segregation tomorrow, segregation forever."

Just two days prior to Wallace's defiant protest, St. Joseph's Mission School implemented reverse integration. Of the 118 students at the school, 106 were Black and 12 were white. There is a historical marker recognizing the white students who were part of the effort to integrate the school. The names of your grandfather, who was in the third grade, and of your great-aunt were two of the names listed. Your grandfather thought that an integrated society was normal even though discrimination lingered in separate water fountains and segregated movie theaters. His best friend was Black but he did not realize how unusual this was for the time. Sadly, it still remains far too infrequent.

As integration of schools became a larger effort in 1971, a number of white families joined the church which was connected to the school to have their children taught by the all-white nuns and teachers. When the principal realized that they were trying to avoid Black teachers teaching their white children, she confronted the families who never attended the church but sent their children to the school. They refused to leave. The complaint from the principal went to the archdiocese and then the Alabama Supreme Court. The principal testified that the families never attended before joining and that they did not attend now. In the end, the church won, so the families had to leave. The principal asked for the students not to be forced to leave until the end of the school year because it was not their fault that their parents were racist. This lady was the first woman to be a principal in the state of Alabama. She was *tov*. She recognized that the efforts to have reverse integration and connection were *tov*. She was your great-grandmother.

Sons, the same DNA that flows from your great-grandmother to me also flows through you. This is who we are as family, even if the shades of our skin are not the same. We are the people who are willing to stand up against the George Wallaces and the other people who do not acknowledge the *tov* of others in the world.

One day, when we visit family in Alabama, we will visit the historical marker for St. Joseph's Mission. The marker notes the effort at reverse integration. This is a form of social integration where the dominant group integrates with the minority or marginalized group rather than vice versa. It was clear for your grandfather and his family that they were in the dominant group. Because you are biracial, it will be unclear to most whether you are in the dominant group or the minority group.

Our experiences will be somewhat similar most of the time. However, in terms of race, this is something I cannot fully understand. That frightens me.

It frightens me because I have seen racism and did not speak up. I did not speak up because the system worked for me. I am afraid that you will have others who act like me near you in those moments when you really need someone to respond like your great-grandmother did. I am trying to equip myself with wisdom and resources to be able to help you in those moments, but I will not have the same experience as you in terms of race.

Sons, you need to know that I did not have to think about the color of my skin for the majority of my life. My first car had Confederate rebel flags on the speaker covers when I bought it (I immediately removed them). At the college I attended in the South, I almost joined a fraternity that sang to the greatness of Robert E. Lee. They claimed that he was their "spiritual founder." The bust of Jefferson Davis moved around campus because he was an alum. I lived in a dorm named after him for half of my undergraduate years. I did not have to think about race and racism. It scares me that, if you had my skin color, I might not feel the need to talk to you about race. Sadly, too many white families do not feel the need to talk about race with their children. Meanwhile, in other families, they have to have "the talk" about race and policing in our country.

The issue of not having to think about race and racism is a huge privilege for me. I am still grappling with what that means. Your grandparents did what most people did in Alabama in the 1970s; they sent a wedding invitation to the governor of the state. He would regretfully decline, but send a cake knife with their names inscribed on it. I realized that I could not use the same wedding cake knife as your grandparents at my wedding. Many couples have a picture of the moment when they cut the cake at their wedding. For us, it would mean George Wallace's name on the side of a knife for a couple of whom he would not approve.

Your mom has helped me expand my appreciation for different types of food. When we go to an Indian restaurant, we are often treated well at the beginning. Then, your mom is often asked where she is from in India. She shares that she was adopted out of Kolkata. Almost instantly, the demeanor of the staff changes because many people, historically and to this day, consider it one of the worst parts of India. This is yet another example of how racism is a devil that destroys the *tov* that binds us all together.

For most of my life, I have been naive to the reality that your parents' skin shades would matter to how people saw us. Your mom and I often joke that she is whiter than me because she likes country music and sometimes has more of a Southern twang than I do. Sadly, too many white people are naive when it comes to how skin color plays a huge role in our lives. There are still a number of people who cannot see how God made us all *tov* and how the connections among us reflect that divine imprint.

Sons, all families have histories. If I am honest, just like every other father, families have a mixture of times when they were on the right side of history and seasons when they were not. I am not claiming that our family has always been on the right side of history, like your great-grandmother was, but I am saying that we, as families, can choose the stories that form us. We get to decide what stays in our family histories, which we can return in difficult times. In essence, this is similar to our relationship with the Bible. The Hebrew scriptures, more so than the Christian Testament, are more honest at "airing out the family's dirty laundry." However, there are plenty of times when scripture wrestles with itself—multiple creation stories, wisdom literature's perspectives on theodicy, Peter and Paul's quarrels, and many more. It is within our tradition to place these stories side by side to tell the reader the larger, unfolding and enfolding story of God. We can pull from the times when our family, tribe, etc. was in the wrong and when we were in the right.

It is important to share with you about the other side of our family. When your mother and I started dating, we shared with each other that we had never dated someone from the other person's ethnicity. We did not say much more than that at the time. However, I recall seeing a picture of your great-grandparents shortly thereafter. I found myself thrilled when I saw your great-grandmother's skin tone (she had very light skin with blue eyes) and your great-grandfather's skin tone (he had almost olive skin with dark hair). I think that many people who are white are afraid of bringing someone home to meet their family who is not white. Thankfully, this was not the case with your grandparents. Sadly, too many people are ridiculed for disturbing the socially constructed purity of a family when their loved one does not fit a particular description.

Science has unequivocally demonstrated that race is not biologically real. It is socially constructed. Said alternatively, it is a human-invented classification system. It was invented by those in power as a way to define physical differences between people. I lived this experience when I left the hospital with you days after your birth. The discharge paperwork for your mother classified her as white. I imagine that the doctors and nurses looked at you and subsequently concluded that she must have been white.

This social construction of race even happened with our friends. When one of you was born, I recall some friends saying that, with your dazzling blue eyes, you were the "whitest biracial baby ever." Prior to that, when your mother and I announced to some close friends that we were engaged, one couple said that we would have beautiful babies because of your mother's "beautiful skin tone" and my "well, very whiteness." Other friends told me that white and Indian biracial children are the most beautiful of all biracial offspring. Even our friends wrestled with what you would look like.

The social construction of race is found within families, friendships, communities, and more. It means different things to different people in different times. Not too long ago, there were classes of races (with those who did the classifying placing themselves at the top, of course). The mixing of the races was seen as being very dangerous, according to those who made the distinctions. To be clear, the image of God resides in all of creation, including all of humanity. Anytime we try to remove that imprint, we are destroying God's image.

The destruction of God's image and the *tov* that God created happens on a regular basis. I know that we will have different experiences with race. I will not be able to comprehend fully what you experience, but you need to know that I am not blind. The scales in front of my eyes have been lifted due to a myriad of reasons, including my marriage to your mother. As your father, I commit to learn more about the experiences that you will face. Too many parents fail to grasp what their children experience in terms of skin color, gender identity, sexual orientation, and much more. The same is true for our neighbors. It is easy to disregard someone else's experiences when they are different from you. Following Jesus means loving your neighbor. That has to include the willingness to admit our blind spots and to learn from the experiences of others.

I believe that we are clay, as the prophet Jeremiah shared many years ago. We are fallible and constantly being formed. Recently, I bought a picture and had it blown up on a metallic finish. Metallic finishes bring out the light in the image with a slight shimmer and rich blacks for better contrast. This finish is durable and resistant to many issues when it comes to artwork. The image that I bought ended up having a scratch on it, so the artist gave me another one for free. Now, that picture hangs in my office and in our bedroom. I am constantly being formed by this picture.

The picture is of the civil rights march from Selma to Montgomery, commonly known as "Bloody Sunday." In 1965, only eighteen years before I was born, people marched from Selma to Montgomery to highlight how some people had more difficulty voting than others. It was a brutal event with beatings and murders. One of those murdered was Rev. James Reeb. The picture that forms me shows Rev. Reeb marching in the front with Dr. King and many others. Rev. Reeb was beaten and died of his wounds in the hospital. Three staunch white segregationists were put on trial for the murder of Rev. Reeb. They were acquitted by an all-white jury. Recently, a fourth man confessed being involved in the murder to NPR journalists. He died less than two weeks after his confession. The murder of Rev. James Reeb remains officially unsolved. Dr. King said that Rev. Reeb's crime was that he dared to live his faith.

Recall that I said that faith is about asking better questions that often do not have answers. I ask myself the following questions and I hope that I always have a clear answer. Am I willing to be in the front of the marching line? Will I show up in those places that others in my tribe find scandalous? Will I fully live out my faith, or will I compromise or buckle when faced with opposition?

My hope and prayer is that I will always answer "yes." I hope to instill these same values in you. Sons, my fear is that someone who is unaware of their socially constructed view of race may treat you in a way that does not honor God's image inherent in you. If that happens, I will be first in the marching line. If I am not around at that point, I hope that I have changed the world such that nobody forgets God's *tov* in themselves and their neighbors.

Because you are *tov*,

Dad

Dear Son,

Racism has been called America's original sin. It is the mistake we can never correct, a transgression whose effects cannot be escaped.

The Declaration of Independence proclaimed that freedom and equality was humanity's natural, God-given state but those professed ideals did not match constructed realities. Slavery was part of the founding DNA of the United States. At our country's beginning, we counted slaves as only three-fifths of a person in our Constitution. Everyone may have been created equal, but they were not recognized as such by the political architects of the early republic. We fought a civil war, passed constitutional amendments, and sought to correct the most egregious injustices of this era. Still, the stain and its ongoing effects remain. It defies any and all attempts to whitewash.

As the historian and legal scholar, Annette Gordon-Reed, poignantly argues, "The most significant fact about American slavery...was its basis in race. Slavery in the United States created a defined, recognizable group of people and placed them outside of society."[14] She notes how the stigma of such separation cannot be undone. Our national story is one of white supremacy and Black inferiority. That lie has been told and believed, acted upon, and perpetuated from the beginning right up to the present moment.

There is a collective awakening about the role that our tragic racial history plays in so many aspects of our contemporary life. People are beginning to explore the way past discrimination and

[14] Annette Gordon-Reed, "America's Original Sin," *Foreign Affairs*, January/February 2018, https://www.foreignaffairs.com/articles/united-states/2017-12-12/americas-original-sin.

past racist economic structures have contributed to the racial wealth gap, which tracks the wide chasm between population demographics and property ownership. From Trayvon Martin to Michael Brown to George Floyd to Breonna Taylor, there is an appalling number of examples indicating something is grotesquely amiss about how our culture enlists law enforcement to police and control non-white members of society. Similar stories could be told about housing, education, transportation, healthcare, and any number of public policy issues. Racism from the far and recent past creates inequities in the present and portends future disparities.

For some, this entire conversation is so overwhelming or even out of bounds that they prefer not to think about it. If evil is not seen, heard, or discussed, then they think its reality can be denied. Others argue that the discussion is inappropriate. The mistakes made centuries or decades ago were committed by other people. Those alive today cannot and should not be held responsible. Besides, there is no way to go back in time and correct the error.

I saw this attitude play out in recent events in the city of Manhattan Beach, California, which is an oceanside suburb of Los Angeles. Early in the twentieth century, an African American couple bought a beachfront resort that became a hot spot for Black tourists. The city government used eminent domain to seize the land, claiming it was needed for developing a public park, and paid the couple a relative pittance for their property. You may not be surprised to learn the park never materialized and the land remained under government control.

Public pressure started to mount on local and state officials to return the land to descendants of the family and to apologize for the government's actions. You could rightly interpret these events as a sign of progress. However, they were not without controversy. While there was broad support for transferring the deed back to the rightful owners, expressing regret for the government's mistake provoked outrage. "If the city were to issue an apology today for what took place 100 years ago," explained one member of the Manhattan Beach City Council, "it would be ascribing the offending events to a vast majority of our residents living here now."[15]

Those alive today do not want to bear responsibility for the transgressions of the past, no matter how egregious they might be or how much they have inadvertently benefitted from them. This perspective views sins as individual actions. It maintains that there are no collective errors, institutional injustices, or structural problems. It believes that the bad apples should be identified and removed but that we should not blame the good apples for being in the same basket with them, especially when the bad apples were in the bucket last season and an entirely new harvest is here now.

While I am skeptical of this view in general, I find it completely unjustifiable as a Christian who believes in the notion of original sin. If our natural disposition is to mess things up, then claiming that past practices and current structures are riddled with injustice is easy to affirm. The harder thing to fathom is the idea that those of us living in the present moment have somehow avoided all the errors of the past.

Original sin is a complicated and contested doctrine. The basic idea is that all human beings make mistakes, that this propensity to error is part of our nature, and that nobody can be perfect. As Bon Jovi explains it in "Blaze of Glory:"

> When you're brought into this world
>
> They say you're born in sin.
>
> Well, at least they gave me something
>
> I didn't have to steal or have to win.

---

[15] Jacey Fortin, "California Beach Seized in 1924 From a Black Family Could Be Returned," *The New York Times*, April 18, 2021, https://www.nytimes.com/2021/04/18/us/bruces-beach-manhattan-california.html.

The teaching has attracted deserved critique for the way it relies on a particular, unsustainable interpretation of the Adam and Eve story in Genesis and draws on outdated biological understandings on what is and is not passed down genetically through the generations. Advances in biblical interpretation and biology have thrown the traditional understanding into doubt. While saving you all the pedantic debates, many faithful Christians have rejected the traditional justifications of this teaching on both scriptural and scientific grounds.

Yet I still find the most famous illustration of original sin's reality to be persuasive. St. Augustine, a theologian and bishop in the early church, wrote a memoir reflecting on his conversion to Christianity. In *Confessions*, he describes being a teenager and conspiring with some of his friends to steal pears from a tree on a neighbor's land. Here is a taste of Augustine's own words:

> We carried off a huge load of pears, not to eat ourselves, but to dump out to the hogs...Doing this pleased us all the more because it was forbidden...Behold, now let my heart confess to [God] what it was seeking there, when I was being gratuitously wanton, having no inducement to evil but the evil itself.[16]

Augustine and his friends took the pears not because they were hungry and had a craving, nor because they knew someone else who was starving and needed the nutrition. They took them simply because they could. With full knowledge that their actions were wrong, they chose to steal the pears anyway simply because there was a thrill in doing what was forbidden.

We do not need to understand all that was going on with Adam, Eve, and the serpent in the Garden of Eden to recognize that this impulse remains with us today. In my own teenage years, my friends and I frequently toilet papered houses for fun.

[16] Saint Augustine, *Confessions*, trans. Henry Chadwick (London: Oxford University Press, 2009).

While the prank was mostly harmless (except for the time our victims had to spend cleaning it up), there was a seduction in the act itself. Doing something "bad" was too tempting to resist. Both committing the prank and, more importantly, getting away with it, brought a rush of good feeling.

Instead of relying on flawed understandings of Genesis, my preferred way of understanding original sin is based on statistics. Humans are not perfect beings. Sometimes we get things right and other times we mess things up. Our goal is always to choose the virtuous path, but inevitably the law of large numbers catches up to us. Eventually, we do something wrong. I do not need the biblical story to explain this particular truth. It just seems obvious from experience. Everybody makes mistakes, sometimes intentionally and at other times innocently. As Reinhold Niebuhr is reported to have written, "[original sin is] the only empirically verifiable doctrine of the Christian faith."[17]

Admitting this leads to an obvious conclusion. If original sin is real, then the things humans create with our lives are marred by imperfections. My thinking on this is not original (pun intended). It was shaped and refined by a piece in *The Christian Century* by an Episcopal theologian named Charles Hefling. He noted that "we—the human species collectively—must own responsibility for constructing cultures, societies, communities, and institutions that encourage the acquisition of some habits and discourage others."[18] In other words, we create structures that shape our lives, sometimes for better and sometimes— because of original sin—for worse.

This means that Christians today cannot ignore the errors of the past, especially the most heinous acts, that reverberate to the present. To do so is to deny the reality of original sin and to compound its force. Flawed humans have been messing things

---

[17] Editorial, *The Christian Century*, June 11, 2014, https://www.christiancentury.org/article/2014-06/unoriginal-sin.

[18] Charles Hefling, "Why we mess things up," *The Christian Century*, June 9, 2014, https://www.christiancentury.org/article/2014-06/why-we-mess-things.

up for a long time. We are inheritors of that legacy, especially in terms of those structures and institutions that give form to our collective life.

None of this sounds particularly controversial. Not all Christians will affirm the doctrine of original sin, and those who do subscribe to it may not embrace my particular understanding of it. Yet most Christians would agree that humans are fallen creatures who struggle to find a way to live with the reality of sin.

Somehow what is easily agreed to in the abstract becomes difficult to accept in the concrete. As I write this letter to you, there is a charged conversation about Critical Race Theory (CRT) that is roiling our nation. Of course, most of the people picking sides in this battle have little understanding of CRT's history, contours, or claims. They have heard talking points on cable news, talk radio, and social media about its purported teachings and they presume those agenda-laden distortions are accurate.

I am far from a CRT scholar. Nor have I widely studied the various writers attempting to use its ideas to analyze American racial dynamics, past and present. My understanding of CRT follows that of Adam Harris, a writer for *The Atlantic* who states, CRT's "proponents argue that the nation's sordid history of slavery, segregation, and discrimination is embedded in our laws, and continues to play a central role in preventing Black Americans and other marginalized groups from living lives untouched by racism."[19]

This alarming insight boils down to a claim that racism in America has historically lingered in our structures and laws in ways that negatively impact the lives of non-white people in our society today. While this idea is disturbing in its consequences, any Christian believing in original sin would find the conclusions

---

[19] Adam Harris, "The GOP's 'Critical Race Theory' Obsession," *The Atlantic*, May 7, 2021, https://www.theatlantic.com/politics/archive/2021/05/gops-critical-race-theory-fixation-explained/618828/.

hard to deny. The sins committed from our country's beginning still influence us today. Once sin enters the world, it tends to spoil everything it touches.

What I think bothers people the most about CRT is the implication that America is an "inherently" or "irredeemably" racist country. If you accept CRT's claims, in this view, then you are committed to the idea that America is beyond saving, which is a difficult thought to embrace among those who see the United States as a "chosen nation" or a "city on a hill." These triumphal and nationalistic beliefs are impossible to reconcile with a society permanently scarred by racism.

To those who transform a nation-state into an idol, this all sounds like heresy. After all, the "god" they are worshiping must be perfect and beyond blemish. For Christians, this is an old and familiar story. Our sin—original and otherwise—puts distance between us and God. It makes us enemies of God, creating a chasm that we cannot close through our own efforts. Reconciliation is beyond our reach. It requires a love and power that comes from beyond us. This gift, which we neither earn nor deserve, is called grace.

I am not sure why Christians, who believe every other sin can only be forgiven through the grace of God, would treat the sin of racism any differently. If CRT teaches us that racism is not something we can heal on our own, then the obvious conclusion —at least to me—is that this is one more opportunity for God's grace to become present, if only we will fully trust in its power.

Jim Wallis, the influential Christian social justice activist, believes this grace that leads to reconciliation can be found in conversation. He lifts up the responsibility of Jesus' followers to help remedy America's original sin of racism not by pretending it will suddenly disappear but by inviting each other into deeper conversation about our own experiences with race. "Only by telling the truth about our history and genuinely repenting of our sins, which still linger," he writes, "can we find the true road to justice and reconciliation."[20] He does not pretend that more conversations solve everything. He is only reminding us that until we first confront the truth, in this case by honestly telling America's racial story, we cannot be set free.

As a young white boy, you, my son, are not personally responsible for the wrongs in our country's past. But you are a beneficiary of the structures that have been built to benefit the dominant group over others. This places on your shoulders an additional burden to know that history so that you can avoid repeating the mistakes, to be aware of how it advantages you and me (and others who look like us) so that we can correct the injustices of the system, and to listen to the stories of those around us who look different from us about their experiences within this nation that are rooted in the color of their skin.

We cannot undo the transgressions of the past. They have influenced the present and will exert a force on the future. But that does not leave us hopeless. Those of us alive in this moment can shed our ignorance and fight to limit the power of this sin today with the goal of creating a more equitable tomorrow. I have every confidence that in committing ourselves to that cause, we will encounter God's redeeming grace and join with the Spirit in doing this holiest of work.

With love,

Dad

---

[20] Jim Wallis, "Racism is 'America's Original Sin.'" *Salon*, January 18, 2016, https://www.salon.com/2016/01/18/racism_is_americas_original_sin_unless_we_tell_the_truth_about_our_history_well_never_find_the_way_to_reconciliation/.

Notes for My Letter about Seeing Color in a World of Black and White

5

The Purpose of Money

Dear Sons,

You never met your great-grandfather, my dad's dad. He was quite a character. As a child, my father moved almost twenty times because grandpa was always buying houses, fixing them up, and then selling them for a small profit. He could have had his own show on HGTV, but he was a man ahead of his time!

In addition to house flipping, he also held a variety of jobs through the years. One of my earliest memories is when Grandpa was a long-haul truck driver. He would be gone for days at a time but he always returned with a present for me and my sister. On one particular occasion he handed us a pack of 1990 Upper Deck baseball cards. Both my love for that sport and my childhood passion for card collecting began on that day.

Looking back, I am suspicious that guilt motivated these gifts. Like many parents or grandparents who are consumed by their jobs at great cost to their families, my grandfather felt bad for being away so often. The pack of baseball cards was a mea culpa for his absence.

Another way he would make amends was by taking us to the store during those lulls when he was not on the road. These trips with grandpa had a ritual element to them. We would first go to the snack bar to eat copious amounts of nachos and cheese. He would regale us with stories about where he had just been and where he was going next. Then, once all the chips were eaten and cheese was gone, we would begin our treasure hunt around the store. My sister and I were each allowed to choose one thing to take home, but our budget was limited to around a dollar. This usually meant that I left the store with more baseball cards or a new Matchbox car.

These trips created an expectation. As a kid, I presumed that going to the store meant coming home with a new toy. You can imagine my surprise when my own dad and I visited the store one day but a present for me was not on his shopping list. After several rounds of bargaining and protest, I declared, "But Dad, it is *only* a dollar!" This seemed like a winning argument to me. Dad just needed a little perspective on the relatively inexpensive nature of my demands. My happiness at his buying this piece of metal and plastic would far exceed the trivial impact on his wallet.

I drastically misjudged how these words would land on his ears.

"Only a dollar?" he asked rhetorically. "Who did the work for that dollar? You don't understand the time and effort required to earn a dollar. Until you have made a dollar of your own, do not ever tell me that something costs *only* anything." My ability to grasp that lesson was a long way off.

My childhood was idyllic. Outside of being denied that Matchbox car on that eventful trip to the store with Dad, I did not want for anything. This is highly surprising in retrospect. With a mom who spent her career as an administrative assistant and a dad who was a carpenter before taking a blue collar job working for our local city government, we were solidly middle class. However, my parents managed to hide from us kids the inevitable financial struggles they faced.

Let me give you two related examples. First, I can remember being told that Dad was no longer going to work on Saturday mornings and this meant our family budget would be a little tighter than usual. Being self-employed, Dad only got paid when he worked. He had no set salary or paid time off. The more hours he put in, the more money he made. Choosing to stop working on the weekends was a trade-off debated by my parents. It allowed for more time as a family, but the cost was a drop in our family income.

Second, we went on a vacation every summer. Looking back, those trips revealed so much. They were never extravagant but we always spent a week exploring a new place. The hotel of choice was a Holiday Inn, selected both because of the modest price and the famed "Holidome" that promised free entertainment and a nice pool. We left the hotel every day at 8 a.m. sharp and would be gone until after dinner that night. Any extra time spent in the room was a waste. Instead, each day was jam-packed with visits to parks, museums, and other fun tourist attractions. After enjoying a meal out, we would return to the hotel exhausted but satisfied, swim for an hour, and then hit the bed so we could do it all again the next day.

Now, as an adult, I realize what was going on. Mom and Dad had saved all year to allow us to go on this trip. The week we spent on vacation were days that Dad was not being paid to fix a roof or remodel a kitchen. My parents wanted to get their money's worth from the experience. We had to make the most of each day because this was truly an extravagance.

I do not want to oversell this story. There were lots of families that were far worse off than us, families that could never dream of an annual vacation. My parents' jobs were steady and they made wise financial decisions all along the way. This is not a tale of barely getting by. Rather, it is an example of two people who worked hard for everything they made and thus were frugal in how they used their hard won resources. Moreover, it is about two parents who repeatedly made great sacrifices for two kids who were largely unaware of the costs incurred on their behalf.

"No one can serve two masters," Jesus preaches to his followers in the Gospel of Matthew, "either you will hate the one and love the other, or you will be devoted to the one and despise the other. You cannot serve both God and money" (6:24).

There are a lot of Christians who fail this test. They are controlled by money. They have turned the dollar into their god. I am not speaking here of those trapped in economic poverty, where limited financial resources restrict opportunity and make life a struggle. I am talking about a different kind of poverty, a spiritual poverty where amassing the biggest pile of money becomes an end in itself.

Logically, this idea has never made sense to me. Money serves two purposes: 1) it facilitates people exchanging goods, and 2) it stores value. Essentially, money can be used for buying things now or to buy things later. The value of money is found in the future possibilities it creates. By itself, money is worthless. Yet many people orient their lives around its accumulation.

Here is a thought experiment. Consider a world where everyone else has disappeared. There is still plenty for you to eat and drink, so those basic needs are met. Many threats of violence and accidents have been eliminated, so you are relatively safe. Since the world has been abandoned, you can pick any house you want. Let us also say that in this imaginary world you have a billion dollars. Sitting in the basement of the home you choose there are pallets of $100 bills. What good is this "fortune" to you? Other than kindling for a fire, the money is worthless because no trading partner exists.

This demonstrates how money's value is in the ways it structures our relationships with others and allows us to have both our needs and wants met through those interactions. I believe this is the key to understanding money. Every dollar you earn and spend is about the connection you have with yourself, with others, and with God. Let me unpack this a bit.

The most precious resource we actually have is not money but time. As mortal creatures, our days are limited. The most pressing challenge we face is determining how to use them well. Unfortunately, few can be bothered to reflect on this fundamental truth. As the stoic philosopher Seneca wrote, "people are frugal in guarding their personal property; but as soon as it comes to squandering time they are most wasteful of the one thing in which it is right to be stingy."

In considering your career path, it is tempting to focus solely on what a job might pay. Many people spend their lives chasing after a bigger paycheck only to arrive at retirement realizing the huge cost of their decision. With one life to live, you will need to reflect deeply on how you want to spend your time. Money should not be the main motivation.

As a teenager, I desperately wanted to make some money over the summer. At the time, the only job you could get legally before turning sixteen was detasseling corn. This involves getting up really early and then spending the day walking through fields pulling out the top of the corn plant. The morning leaves you completely soaked from the dew that has gathered overnight and by the afternoon you are baking in the hot sun. It is hard, miserable work.

My mom strongly discouraged me from taking the job. Not only did she understand what was involved from doing it during her own childhood, she wanted me to enjoy being a kid. She knew the chance to have a summer free of obligation was a luxury in short supply, but I lacked the perspective to appreciate her wisdom. I took the job, made a little bit of money, but lost an entire summer of fun.

Allocating our time is a hugely consequential aspect of our lives. Money cannot be the dictator that determines how your days are spent. But, of course, this guidance is offered from a place of relative privilege and comfort. There are lots of people whose days are consumed by a job (or jobs) they hate because their financial circumstances and our economic realities compel them to work. Bills have to be paid and mouths have to be fed regardless of how the worker feels about the job to be done. Labor should be respected, not denigrated. The issue is the number of people in our world forced to toil because our economic system restricts their ability to choose their own path. The need to subsist becomes a hindrance to their freedom and self-determination.

The ways we use money can uphold or undermine this system. It can exacerbate or improve the financial struggles of others. For example, studies have found that only about 30 percent of hotel guests leave a tip for the housekeeping staff. These workers are often poorly compensated for the grueling work they do to make guests comfortable. A tip both dignifies their efforts and increases the amount of money in their pocket.

One of the joys in my life is regularly giving back to the educational institutions that equipped me for vocational success. By forming my mind and character, they prepared me to lead and allowed me to pursue the professional opportunities that have been so personally meaningful. I was lucky to have parents who helped shoulder this financial burden, but many other families are not in a position to do the same. Sacrificing some of my own resources to give others the chance at a life-changing education is my way of paying things forward.

On a larger scale, you should also see money as a vehicle for creating an economic system that is fairer for all. From supporting businesses and companies that produce products and treat their employees ethically to supporting organizations and political candidates advocating for public policies that enhance opportunities for everyone, you can use the resources you have to play a role in creating more equitable relationships across our society. That may sound lofty and idealistic until you realize there are powerful interests benefitting from the status quo who use their own financial resources in exactly the same way but for far more nefarious ends.

Indeed, I have come to understand justice as being about right relationships. This idea is not original to me but I also do not remember where I first heard it. A just world is one where all of us live in right relationship with each other, with creation, and with God. Money can be a means by which we realize that justice. We can use it to correct and create these right relationships. Alternatively, it can be used to distort our connections with each other by advantaging some and oppressing others.

Christians often miss how frequently and emphatically Jesus talks about money. He wants our loyalty and trust to be fully invested in God. He recognizes that money can be transformed into an idol, drawing us away from God and tempting us to pursue wealth at any and all costs. Such distortions create vast injustices.

At one point in the gospels, a man approaches Jesus and asks, "Teacher, what good deed must I do to inherit eternal life?" Jesus counsels the man to follow the law and he claims to have done so. "What do I still lack?" he asks. Then Jesus confronts him more directly, "If you wish to be perfect, go, sell your possessions, and give the money to the poor, and you will have treasure in heaven; then come, follow me." The man walks away sad because he had such great wealth (Matthew 19:16–22 NIV).

What this story makes clear is how often our pursuit of money and high value of material things gets in the way of our relationship with God. Money is supposed to be the means to an end, a vehicle for pursuing our goals. The working out of God's justice—living in right relationship with God, each other, and our environment—should be our aim.

As 1 Timothy states, "Those who want to get rich fall into temptation and a trap and into many foolish and harmful desires that plunge people into ruin and destruction. For the love of money is a root of all kinds of evil. Some people, eager for money, have wandered from the faith and pierced themselves with many griefs" (6:9–10 NIV).

While the circumstances of the original audience were far different than ours, the wisdom of this passage remains the same. When money becomes our chief love, then we find our souls disfigured and our actions contributing to the harm of others. Yet, when our resources are used to help others flourish as God intends, then we become heralds of the Divine Reign that is defined by equitable and enduring relationships.

The true value of a dollar is known when our money is used as a witness to God's justice.

Steadfast in hope,

Dad

Dear Sons,

Fatherhood does not wait until someone is ready. When I shared with a mentor that I was going to be a dad, he told me that fatherhood really did not start until the child turned three. "Then," he said, "it gets to be fun and you can do stuff with them." This statement puzzled me at first and now, after some reflection, I find myself even more bothered by the comment. Fatherhood does not start when the child reaches a certain age. For me it started when I first looked into your eyes in the hospital nursery and echoed a voice from ages past, "You are my son with whom I am well pleased" (Matthew 3:17). In that moment, God said that Jesus was his son. When I first locked eyes with you, I likewise claimed you as my own. Our relationship did not hesitate. As this relationship was embarking, I saw the need to be your teacher concerning a variety of topics, including money.

Money is an important topic in our family. My parents encouraged me to go through financial classes, such as those with Dave Ramsey. Each time we listened to him on the radio, we would have a discussion about how we tell money what to do so that it does not tell us what to do. In the moment, I did not always enjoy it, but my parents were intentional when it came to talking about money. The goal was never to get rich. Instead, it was to be able to support our family.

As I learned more about money, I learned that it carries more than its value. Due to a drug addiction, a member of our family stole money from my grandparents. It was devastating. From that moment, money became emotional. It carried the pain of betrayal. That person never fully apologized for their actions. Therefore, when questions about money come up, I am very sensitive to what it is communicating. I can feel this tension in my veins. Sons, you never know what hurt someone is carrying when you discuss money with them.

I mowed a plethora of lawns when I was young. As soon as I was paid, I would often give the money to my mother to put in my savings account. I loved seeing my balance grow and thinking about what I could buy. I learned the beauty of compounding interest when I was young; it either works for you or against you. Banks benefit from your deposits. Therefore, they honor your money with a small additional amount of money. That money can keep growing and building upon itself.

Of course, the opposite is true when you owe money to someone or an entity as those debts can keep multiplying. Many of my friends learned financial lessons the hard way through struggles with credit debt and other money-related stress. Thankfully, my parents were wise guides and taught me well.

I enjoy taking you to the store and showing you how much money we have for buying seeds. Unlike most kids who make a beeline for the toy section, you prefer investing money in things that grow. A great example of this is planting your favorite fruit—tomatoes. If you plant one seed, it has the capacity to bring forth hundreds of seeds from all of the tomatoes that it produces.

One of the ways that I want to teach you is to offer you compound interest that financial institutions used to offer generously. I want to show you that if you plant your money in savings, it will grow. It will be there when the storms come, and it will allow you to not have to work as much simply to pay for compound interest that is working against you. Therefore, sons, I commit to paying you generous interest payments for money that you put in a savings account. I want you to enjoy seeing the numbers grow and imagining what you can do with it if you keep saving.

Because I saved throughout my childhood, I was only fourteen years old when I put a down payment on my first car—a 1971 Chevelle SS. I loved that car. Your grandfather taught me so much about life under the hood of that car. I had to take a loan out from my parents—your grandparents—for the rest of the cost of the car. I recall seeing a notebook with lots of numbers and payments of $20. I enjoyed seeing those numbers become smaller and smaller. I was fortunate that my parents could give me a loan, teach me about money, and not charge too much interest. I learned this value from my parents, I shared it with your uncles when they lived with us, and now I will share it with you.

Unfortunately in life, not all debts are equally desired. The summer before turning twelve, I was in the front yard working on my baseball swing. Well, if I am being honest, it was closer to a bunt. Instead of trying to hit the ball, I would simply nudge it a few feet and then run to first base. Despite my mother's warnings, the unexpected happened. I got ahold of a pitch and sent the ball sharply into right field, which turned out to be our dining room. The double paned window in the front of our house fell victim to my newfound status as a slugger. This was not going to be cheap to replace.

My parents helped me set up a way to repay them for the window through a long list of chores spread out over a few months. A week later, we went to a family friend's house for their Kentucky Derby party. It is always a fun and exciting time. The adults would bet on the horses after studying the odds and reading about them.

Meanwhile, my grandmother innocently gave me three dollars to be able to participate. She wanted all of us—including the kids—to be able to join in on the screaming and excitement that seems to last about two minutes while spectators at the event are wearing funny hats. I had no idea which horse to choose. I ended up choosing the horse with the coolest name: Thunder Gulch. This horse had some of the worst odds (24.5 to 1) in the derby. As the race began, everyone was screaming for the beautiful creatures galloping around the track as they chased a fake animal running ahead of them on the rail. When the race ended, many folks were furious with the results. I had no idea who won the race but it was fun to watch. Suddenly, my grandmother came over to me and told me that my horse had won the Kentucky Derby despite some of the worst odds ever!

Amazingly, my prize was just enough to pay for the window that I had obliterated. I began to celebrate because the sweetness of my victory meant liberation from my parents' chore list. My mother did not share in my delight. To her this was an opportune moment to teach me about the role of luck and the dangers of betting as a financial strategy. She got down on her knees, looked me in the eyes, and said that I was "lucky, but I should never count on luck to fix my mistakes." Her caution was warranted, as usually the odds are stacked against you in gambling, unlike investments such as the stock market that generally have a history of positive returns.

Sons, as much as I enjoy seeing the numbers in my savings account go up and the numbers in my loans go down, it is not about the numbers. It is about what money allows us to do. All of our harvest is a gift from God to be shared and enjoyed. Tithing your money and possessions allows you to do some pretty amazing things. This is why I encourage you each year to tithe your toys away. By giving away ten percent of your toys, we accomplish many things. First, you please your parents who dislike clutter. Second, you can only play with so many toys at once. Third, you hoarding toys means that another child does not have enough. Tithing your toys ensures that the world is more like God intended. I practice tithing my possessions as well. It works best in the years when I do not buy as many shirts that I tithe to charity. After all, I can only wear one shirt at a time. If I hoard it, someone else does not have a shirt. I have noticed that tithing my possessions also makes me more hesitant to buy things. This, in turn, means that there is more room to play with toys in the house and that closets are not stuffed to the point that you cannot find what you are looking for.

Sons, as much as I enjoy seeing my bank account go up, I also find delight in seeing the numbers go down. Recently, we started using a website through which people could donate towards your birthday gift. The website enables you to choose a variety of charities to which to give half of your donations. The owners of the website receive a small percentage for their service. You get the remaining funds on a gift card to choose a gift for yourself. The point is that you can see the good that you can do with money.

Instead of more plastic ending up in landfills, you are able, for example, to feed members of our community who are hungry and help build playgrounds for children. This is the purpose of money. With money, you can help make the world more like God dreams for it to be—from the dinner table to the playground.

For many of us, money is about power. It is about being able to control our surroundings, including our loved ones. Such use of money leads to a life in which you never feel you have enough. You are always trying to make more because you want more toys, but then you need a bigger house to hold those toys. The cycle just keeps going. This is an old concept known as scarcity. It is deadly and destroys joy.

Jesus often dealt with people who embodied the notion of scarcity. They could never have enough so they had to build silos to store it all. Today, we call these storage units, one of the fastest growing industries in the country. The purpose of money is not to be able to store your stuff in a place where it collects dust, moths destroy, and it takes twenty minutes just to get to the locked door that holds your stuff.

Sons, when I moved away from my parents to go to college, I had to sell my Chevelle. I loved that car. I loved the way it idled, the smell of the exhaust, and the heat that came up from above the transmission through the floorboard. We decided to meet the new owner halfway between our homes at a Cracker Barrel in Cullman, Alabama. Your grandfather drove his 1969 Chevrolet Camaro convertible. I drove my Chevelle. We raced down back roads the entire way there, just like we had done so many times before. When we arrived, my father was already talking to the

Chevelle's soon-to-be new owner. I had sunglasses on to cover my eyes because they were bloodshot after crying during the entire drive over my impending loss. My father took one look at me and chuckled. Then he reminded me that I was destined to be a preacher and that required setting material things aside.

I have never disagreed with my dad more. He looked at the car and saw three thousand plus pounds of metal painted red with black stripes. I saw all the memories that car had made possible. There was my dad's best friend from high school helping us put the engine back under the hood after another friend had helped us rebuild it. Sadly, both of those guys had passed away but that engine lived on. I still remember tightening the last engine bracket screw of my Chevelle as I looked up at my dad from underneath the car, which only took us eight hours. I was letting go of more than a car; I was releasing the bonding experience of countless nights working with Dad as he opened the world of muscle cars to his millennial son. I was grieving the loss of all that car represented about a chapter of my life that was coming to a close. Yet that chapter was written only because of the lessons my parents had taught me about money. I hope that I can guide you in the same ways.

Sons, money allows us to have moments in which relationships can be forged. Money allows us to bring a similar type of joy to someone who has not had a hot meal in a week. Money allows us to bring a similar joy to children on a playground. Money is not about numbers; it is about the life and experiences that it enables. The storms will come and, sometimes, our bunts will be a double into the gap. Yes, sometimes, a horse with a cool name wins to wipe away our mistakes. I will do my best to show you that money is similar to planting a garden. It is not solely about the harvest. It is about the joy of seeing the fruit of your labor in your backyard or under the hood.

Without hesitation,

Dad

Notes for My Letter about the Purpose of Money

6

The Man God Hopes You Will Be

Dear Son,

I thought my days of fighting bullies were over once I left the school playground, but they keep showing up spoiling for a brawl, even in the places that I think are the safest. As the senior pastor at a local church which chartered Cub and Boy Scouts troops, I had to sign some documents each year. Beyond that, there was little in terms of expectations of me. However, I do not believe in relationships where I do the bare minimum. I found ways to be involved with the organization.

Everything changed in 2014 when there was an issue of bullying within the troop. There was one scout who had misconduct issues. The adults saw the benefit of the program to this scout, so some adults did not want to act. He crossed a line when he began to bully other kids in the troop. It became clear that the son acted as the father did. His father was a bully. The father cussed out the Scoutmaster in front of the youth and the adults. At this time, my signature was not the only action that was required of my position. I, as the head of the charter, was the only person who could dismiss someone—adult or youth—from the troop.

I sought more information about the situation before taking any action. The council became involved. They requested a meeting with me and some of the local leaders. At the meeting, there was a myriad of excuses to defend the father and son. This included the fact that the father was in the military, so bullying is "normal." Finally, someone from the council said that Scouts prepare boys to be men where there will be lots of bullying, so they need to get used to it.

Son, there are times in life when you have to look inside your soul to see if you are ready to try to make a difference. I knew that I had to do something, not because of my title or position, but because if I did not, I would not be able to look at myself in the mirror.

My response began with a "no" and a long pause. Sometimes, son, all you can say is "no" or "woah." In these moments, you will echo Jesus in Luke 11 and Matthew 23 in addition to other voices in scripture. You are saying that what is happening is not right and that there is something at stake if things do not change. I do not know how you will address conflict in your life. My hope, son, is that you will be a lover, not a fighter, but be willing to fight for what you love—on the playground, with your family, at work, and throughout the world.

After the pause, I said that bullying is "not normal." I added that I was bullied a lot growing up. I knew that pain. I still know that pain from time to time, even in the church where there is bullying. I declared that the troop would not prepare boys to deal with bullying in the world. Instead, our troops would shape the boys and young men into change agents in a world where bullying needs to cease. I would not allow bullying by adults or kids in "my troop."

Son, men have traveled across oceans displacing people and planting their country's flag in soil and calling it theirs. As men, we need to address our tendency to want to dominate and subdue the earth and others. Yet, somewhere in my gut, I believe that claiming ownership can be a good thing. I do not know if I would have been able to say "no" if I had not taken ownership or at least a vested interest in what was transpiring. It is for this reason that I call you "mine" because of our relationship which makes me "your dad."

Son, you will need to claim things in life. These claims are not meant to take things from others, but to say that you have a voice and that you feel called to make a difference. As men, it can be easy for us to sit on the sidelines because we know that the game of life typically works to our benefit. This is particularly true for me as a white man. Things for you will be more complicated.

To some, you will look white and can have, as they say at graduations, "all of the rights, privileges, and responsibilities appertaining thereto." To others, your skin will not look pure enough. You will not fit their category because your parents are not both white.

Son, you need to know that there will be some people who do not approve of your parents being married because we cannot pass for being the same socially-constructed race. I do not simply want to prepare you for a world of bullying. I promise to be a change agent, and I hope that you will be as well. Nobody can tell your mom and dad who they can marry and love. Nobody should do that for another person. I will always celebrate whom you love and will love them as well. I will do this because I love what you love because you are made of me. Further, in some sacred way, I am made of you more and more each day.

While being married to your mom has been the greatest joy of my life, you need to know that we do not always fit in people's categories. Once, after meeting Mom a few times, a neighbor came over to drop off some guacamole (which I will always have difficulty sharing). They mistook your mom as my "maid." This was an incredibly hurtful situation for us. I found myself wrestling with common stereotypes and assumed gender roles. I wondered if the neighbor would have thought that your mom was my maid if she had been white. In another instance, when Mom first came back with me to Alabama to meet my family, the pastor at my home church introduced your mom to the entire church as "my friend." This made my entire family upset. I think that it helped all of us understand what we tend to ignore for the sake of our own comfort. These are difficult conversations that I have been forced to have with people around me because of what is going on inside them. The problem is theirs not ours.

Son, I hope that you will seek to understand before being understood. In some sacred way, it opens doors to new possibilities. Plus, you will be in good company as Jesus was thought to be the gardener at the resurrection scene in John 20. If there is to be a birth from above for all of us, it will involve people revising their priorities, as a Sunday school teacher at my church says. I do not want you to carry the burden alone for what other people think. Son, I want you to believe that you can always make a difference regardless of your title or position.

When I was a freshman in high school, I met my best friend from childhood. To honor his confidentiality and be aware that whom he loves might cause him issues, I will call him Mike. We quickly became best friends as we were in a class that was bravely taught by a woman who had been my mother's favorite teacher when she went to the same high school years earlier. This class was called "Introduction to Business Careers." There were over twenty, mostly freshman, young men in this class. There was one young lady. For the teacher, it was chaos and a battle each day. The teacher valiantly tried to keep some semblance of order.

Sadly, we still expect only men or only women to be in some situations—like this business classroom. I am working on this situation. I hope that it will not be the same when you are almost forty. This is yet one more place where men need to be change agents.

Back in that classroom, pre-cut carrots would be sent shooting across the room when the teacher turned her back to the group to write on the board. To remedy the situation, the teacher found ways to have others write on the board in order for her always to keep watch. Then, some students brought lasers to class to bother others across the room. The teacher began to look for the lasers. The young men kept adapting their tactics to continue to be a problem for the teacher.

I noticed that Mike began being bullied in that classroom. It bothered me because when you are close to someone, their pain and struggle is yours. It is how men need to take ownership instead of being the ones causing the pain and struggle. Mike, eventually, told me that he was being bullied because he was gay. He was the first person to tell me that he was gay. I was blind to his experience, but, through a lot of work, I began to better understand his pain and struggle.

Two months later, my grandmother had an aneurysm. She died a few days later. She was extremely formative for me in my life. I spent countless nights at my Granny and Poppy's house. I asked Mike to pray for her. Mike shared that he was sad to hear about my grandmother, but that he would not pray for her because he was atheist. Growing up in Alabama, I had never heard someone say that they were atheist. Our friendship moved quickly in four months. I learned many ways in which my best friend was different from me. In that same span of time, Mike said that he was going to drop out of high school.

It was during this freshman year of high school that I began to have a sense of my call to ministry. In our tradition, it meant that I needed to obtain a master's degree. Meanwhile, my best friend told me that he was atheist, gay, and going to drop out of high school. What was I supposed to do in this situation?

Son, there are times to form your identity over and against something or someone. Yet, I hope that you will more often form your identity with and for something or someone.

My experience with church was that it was a community of people who loved and formed me. My family had been going to the same local church for four generations. I was an insider, so the community worked for me. Mike's experience was the polar opposite.

Mike's experience of church was of people talking about how those like him deserved to go to hell and burn for eternity. He shared stories with me of how people at my high school seemed to care about him, but then he came to realize that it was just a ploy to get him to go to their church. At that time, there were three big churches where it was popular to go. They were always "battling for souls." Mike, understandably, had no interest in a community where he would always be an outsider.

A year later, I gave my first sermon at my home church. I spoke about what it meant to be a "Jesus Freak," which was an album by one of my favorite Christian bands at the time. A book with the same title followed. I spoke about the need for our congregation to be Jesus Freaks as we love other people. I shared the word for love in a variety of languages. As I preached in the overwhelmingly large pulpit at my home church, I looked down to see my youth pastor supporting me. I looked in the pews to see my family and Sunday school teachers in amazement that the boy who had to be dragged to church suddenly felt called to be a preacher. I looked up in the balcony. To my great surprise, Mike was there.

This was the only time that Mike came to hear me preach. He sat as far away from others as possible. Mike had someone hand him their bulletin because he snuck into the sanctuary so fast that a greeter did not see him to offer a bulletin. Even though he only came once, I always imagine that Mike—someone who is the opposite of me in many ways *and* my best friend to this day—is always in the balcony. Son, my hope for you is that you will always be aware of who is in the balcony sitting as far away as possible in order to be safe.

In the founding location of our church denomination, there is a large meeting house (sanctuary). Now, there is a protective stone barrier to help preserve the wooden structure. I went to college down the street from it. We took trips to stand in the holy space. Each time we went, I could not help but think about the balcony. I wondered if Mike would have sat there. Historically, it was a place for slaves to sit while their white masters sat down below.

Son, there will always be people in the balcony. It is these moments when you have to look inside of your soul to see if you are ready to make a difference. I pray that you will make a difference, not because of your title, position, or guilt, but because you have the power in this situation. You can use it for the benefit of others to speak for justice. This act, just as the large meeting house, is the message that needs to be preserved in stone.

Son, I have experienced numerous times when the communities in which I am an insider questioned if I was really a part of the tribe. This was not due to the color of my skin, but because I did not repeat the same broken lines to maintain the categories. To be clear, the maintenance of such categories benefits someone like me—a straight, white man. Put differently, tribes tend to become enraged when they hear that they are not the only beloved tribe. As I often point out, Galileo was deemed a heretic because he told people that they were not the center of the universe! Still, taking the Way of Jesus means to lift up the voices of those who are in the balcony.

Son, I promise always to be a change agent with and for you. I promise to say "no" when it needs to be said. In this way, I refuse to outsource fatherhood to others. It is my responsibility and honor.

As I wrestle with the man that God hopes you will be, my fervent prayer is that you will be someone who can look himself in the mirror knowing that you seek to overturn the systems, especially when they work for you. I realize that you will never look like a "mini me"—and that is good. I want you to be a beautiful mix of your mother and me. My dream is that you will be a lover, not a fighter, and a change agent rather than someone who does the bare minimum of what is expected of you in life. Son, my honest fear is that the same struggles that I am trying to overcome and overturn will be yours. Unfortunately, men usually just adjust their tactics instead of embodying the needed change. Yes, there will be people in the balcony, but I hope that they are not the same for you as they were for me. I hope that if you have children one day, you can say the same to them.

With great hope,

Dad

Dear Sons,

The first memory I have is from preschool. I remember playing carefree in the basement of a Lutheran Church alongside other kids and then Mom picking me up. It was all routine. As a four-year-old, my biggest concern was about getting lunch. I certainly did not stop to consider what might have been going on inside my mother's head that day.

That moment feels different now that I am the parent and you are just turning three. You are not inside my head. You cannot comprehend what I am thinking. But I regularly wonder what the future holds for you. I watch you just beginning to understand how the world works and find myself fearful of how soon your precious innocence will be lost. After you fall asleep, I lie beside you trying to imagine your future. The routine moments are laden with the possibilities and worries about what is yet to come.

Sometimes your mom and I will share in this conversation. Like other parents, we worry about mistakes we might be making or whether we are doing everything possible to set you up for success in the future. No doubt a lot of this borders on the ridiculous.

The other day I arrived to pick you up from daycare. Your teacher pulled me aside to share a concern. I could tell from the serious look in her eyes that something unusual had occurred. Apparently, you and your best friend at daycare both wanted the same red truck. Instead of finding a way to share, you acted out of anger and put your hands on your friend's neck.

Your mom and I were mortified. We were momentarily convinced that your life had taken a dark turn and we quickly had to course correct or risk losing you to a path of delinquency and violence. This sounds hyperbolic but on that particular night this was how we felt.

We responded harshly. You received a scolding in the car from me and another at home from Mom. There was a lengthy time out and then more chastisement. We made you "write" a note of apology to your friend (it was really just some scribbles by you and a lengthier note penned by us). We profusely told your friend's parents how sorry we were and assured them we were taking corrective action.

Once we gained our bearings, perspective set in. Every young kid struggles to share, which is why so many children's books and TV shows cover the topic. You went right back to playing with your friend (and he with you), which reveals both your short memory and the underlying truth about your relationship with him. We may have overreacted.

Honestly, it is hard not to see what you become as reflecting on ourselves. If you enjoy wild success, then (we like to think) that's a reflection of our parenting. Alternatively, if you struggle through life, that says something else. So many parents live vicariously through their children while taking blame or credit for the shape of their kids' lives.

Science tells a much more complicated story. The psychology professor Yuko Munakata, describes how, "studies have followed identical twins and fraternal twins and plain old siblings growing up together or adopted and raised apart. Growing up in the same home does not make children noticeably more alike in how successful they are, how happy or self-reliant they are, and so on."[21]

These findings let parents off the hook. Parents are not responsible for how the kids turn out. If nothing we do matters, then it does not matter what we do, right?

[21] Yuko Munakata, "Why parents should stop blaming themselves for how their kids turn out," *IDEAS.TED.COM*, January 12, 2021, https://ideas.ted.com/why-parents-should-stop-blaming-themselves-for-how-their-kids-turn-out/.

Dr. Munakata reaches a different conclusion. "These findings are not all that shocking when you think about how the same parent can shape different children in different ways. For example, one child might find it helpful when her mother provides structure, while her sister finds it stifling." She adds, "just because an event doesn't shape people in the same way doesn't mean it had no effect."

So, your mom and I are working to be gentler on ourselves when it comes to shouldering the responsibility for determining your future. We trust that our love and attention, our providing you with unique experiences and constant support, will prove valuable regardless of what direction your life heads. We are working to let go of the idea that the smallest mistake will doom you.

The other day your mom turned to me and said, "I just want him to be kind." That seems like the perfect goal for a parent when it comes to raising a child. No pressure to develop a specific passion or excel in a specific way. There is no expectation around the type of kid you should be or the adult you should become. It is simply the desire that, regardless of what you do, there is a certain character that can be developed to guide you in situations such as when someone else wants your red truck.

In his book *In Defense of Kindness*, the pastor Bruce Reyes-Chow writes that, "to be kind is to accept that each person is a created and complex human being—and to treat them as if you believe this to be true."[22] I join your mom in wishing that kindness will be one of your defining traits.

This definition succinctly conveys the key elements of seeing another person as human. Each of us is a created being. Like a potter, God molds us and shapes us, making our lives into a work of divine art (Isaiah 64:8). Failing to notice this about another person reduces their dignity. If we deny their created status, then we refuse to see their existence as being connected to God. We ignore the most essential part of their being.

---

[22] Bruce Reyes-Chow, *In Defense of Kindness* (St. Louis: Chalice Press, 2021).

In a similar vein, the human person is innately complex. Each of us has a wide diversity of emotions, desires, and experiences. None of us interprets each situation the same way. All of us are motivated by different goals. Our perspective in any one situation is influenced by our past.

Serving as a congregational pastor taught me just how complex human beings could be. I came to realize how even a collection of humans worshiping and sharing life together before God can all operate with very different understandings of what is "normal" or "acceptable" or "right." A lot of conflict within churches, families, workplaces, and so forth is not the result of people acting maliciously but people simply operating out of their varying conceptions of what is normal that naturally come into tension with each other.

Practicing kindness is a struggle because we want to reduce people to something less than a person. We either want to ignore their createdness or their complexity. Treating someone as kind involves recognizing both the sacredness of their life and honoring its complexity.

Looking back on my life thus far, my own parents were exceedingly kind. The kindness of your grandparents is seen in a gift they shared with your aunt and myself. Neither of my parents went to college. They both started working right out of high school, my mom as a bank secretary (as it was called then) and my dad as a carpenter. Both of them found meaning in their careers and made a difference in our local community, but neither of them chose their paths after exploring a range of options.

Over the course of their careers, they went to work every day and saved every dollar they could. They raised two kids, imparting in us the belief that the world was wide open to us. I grew up confident in a future where anything was possible. When we graduated high school, they made it financially possible for both of us first to attend college and then to go on to graduate school.

Their generosity was an act of kindness. Because of the value our parents placed on our lives, they made countless sacrifices along the way. There were personal indulgences small and large foregone to make our education possible one day. They believed education was the path to exploring the complexities of our lives and to discovering God's vocational call. My parents provided your aunt and me with an opportunity they never had: the gift of spending our lives doing what we love.

I was lucky. My mom and dad had incredible foresight and made considerable sacrifices to achieve their goals. For various reasons many parents are not able to practice kindness towards their own kids in the same way. Covering the ever rising costs of a college education is beyond the means of many families.

Still, a critical part of parenting is being kind. It entails treating your child as the created and complex being that they are by encouraging them to grow comfortable in their own skin, pursue their own dreams, and chart their own course through life.

This can be difficult to practice. We parents have strong ideas about what our kids should become. As I sorted out my own call into ministry, I remember informing my dad that the scholarship support I received from our denomination and the financial backing of my parents left me feeling liberated. While others would be burdened by student debt, I would not carry such an onerous weight after graduation. This meant that I could take any pastorate, perhaps even one that paid relatively poorly. My parents' generosity in providing for my education meant I could take a much less lucrative job.

He was not impressed. I could see the wheels turning in his head. The whole point of paying my way through college was to help my career take off. It was not to subsidize a vow of poverty. I do not recall his exact response but I remember he managed to hold his tongue despite his obvious skepticism.

Frederick Buechner, a well-known spiritual writer worthy of your attention, once said, "the place God calls you is the place where your deep gladness and the world's deep hunger meet."[23] This far more beautifully describes what I poorly conveyed to my own dad. There are needs in the world that require our involvement. There are gifts and skills each of us possess. The trick to finding our vocations is lining them up. We feel most alive, most fully ourselves, when our energies are invested in what brings us great joy *and* when our efforts tangibly improve the lives of others.

I might be stretching this kindness thing a little far but Buechner is basically saying, "God wants us to be kind to ourselves and kind to others." By attending to the ways our own createdness and complexities can respect and honor the same in others, we fulfill our divine callings.

All this is to say that your mom and I look at you now with great wonder. We marvel at what you might become, at where life might take you. We are eager to encourage your deep gladness and to help you identify how it might intersect with the world's deep hunger. We pray that we will be role models in teaching you how to practice kindness.

We already find ourselves taking pride in you regardless of what form your life ultimately takes. What matters is not what you become but who you are. We are working hard to resist setting unfair expectations. We are proud simply because you are our son. We are confident all the rest will take care of itself and wherever the journey leads will be beautiful because you are the one walking it.

Here again, I catch myself tripping over words. This delight that I find in you—this pleasure I derive from your success and accomplishments—is something the Bible discourages. Proverbs famously warns that, "pride goes before destruction, a haughty spirit before the fall" (16:18). Thinking too highly of one's self is debilitating because it blinds us to our failings. We fail to notice our shortcomings, and left unattended, they become our ruin.

---

[23] Frederick Buechner, *Wishful Thinking* (New York: HarperOne, 1993).

Even more sharply the book of James describes the proud as an "enemy" of God. It quotes a different verse in Proverbs saying, "God opposes the proud but shows favor to the humble" (4:6). Inflated egos get in the way of God's purposes. Thus, they warrant God's judgment. Humility is required to stay in right relationship, to keep the right perspective on things.

Parents tend to ignore these biblical teachings when it comes to their own kids. Pride may generally be bad, but how could they not be proud of their own child? Not taking that pleasure in their offspring seems cruel. It feels unnatural, even trauma-causing. Parents beam with pride and kids earnestly want to make their parents proud.

I discovered the way out of this puzzle one Sunday in worship when you were quite young. We were sitting together and the congregation began to sing, "Take my life, and let it be.[24]" The verses of that hymn are in the first person. The words leaving our lips are meant to convey a desire about our own individual lives.

That morning, I held you as we sang.

Take my life and let it be consecrated Lord to Thee.

Take my moments and my days, let them flow in ceaseless praise.

You smiled and clapped.

Take my hands and let them move at the impulse of Thy love.

Take my feet and let them be swift and beautiful for Thee.

You danced and dreamed.

Take my will and make it Thine, it shall be no longer mine.

Take my heart, it is Thine own, it shall be Thy royal throne.

---

[24] "Take My Life and Let It Be," by Frances Ridley Haverhal [PD].

I was singing (off key) about you that morning. Those words became a prayer that you would take all of your life and offer it up to God. My pride is rooted in the hope and the certainty, in the confidence and the conviction, that the Lord will use it in beautiful ways.

I am proud because God used my life to make me your father. I will be proud of any and every way God chooses to use your moments and your days.

Take my son and he will be ever, only, all for Thee.

With unending love,

Dad

Notes for My Letter about the Man God Hopes You Will Be

7

Promises to Keep

Dear Sons,

As a pastor, I go to a lot of weddings. More specifically, I preside at a lot of weddings. The couple may be the star of the show, but like a key background actor in Hollywood, the minister plays an essential role in the performance. I am the one who signs the marriage certificate that makes everything official.

Obtaining my signature requires the couple to do a lot of work. I put them through a process called "pre-marital counseling." That word—counseling—scares people off at first. They imagine sorting out their deepest problems or their complicated relationships with their parents in front of their soon-to-be spouse. Or even worse, they fear having to talk about sex with a pastor (because that too is part of marriage).

These fears are misplaced. All that such counseling involves is a series of conversations designed to ensure they enter marriage in a healthy way and with a common set of expectations. But there is one strong admonition I give to every couple that comes under my care, a moment where my voice grows a little stern, as I issue this ritual warning:

> On your wedding day, you have no idea how the future will unfold. The promises you make at the altar are

about being there for each other, no matter what transpires. Joy is sure to find you but there will also be times that try your souls. Moments will come that tempt you to compromise on your commitments.

Here, I pause for emphasis. I want the couple to grasp how serious they should take all this. Then I continue:

Nobody is forcing you to make this promise. If you neither mean these words nor intend to honor them, then do not insult everyone there, especially your future spouse, by pretending otherwise. Above all, do not mock God with such a blatant lie. However, if your pledge is sincere, then you must do whatever it takes to uphold it in the years ahead.

While that advice is specifically about marriage, it speaks to promises in general. The same logic applies to bringing a child into this world. Your arrival created a set of moral obligations that your mom and I strive every day to meet. These commitments were freely made. Each dawn brings a new opportunity for us to follow through on them.

Different parents interpret these promises in various ways. My own dad had a friend who believed that his responsibility ended when his children turned eighteen. Perhaps jokingly, he claimed that the day after their birthday party he was going to change the locks on the house. The message was not subtle. To him there was a clear point at which his obligations ceased, or at least changed substantially.

Such a view appalls me.

There is no doubt our relationship will evolve over the years, but promises are not like contracts. They do not end on an exact date or conclude when specific terms have been met. They are more like the biblical concept of a covenant, where commitments are made and both parties trust each other to follow through regardless of the passage of time or the bleakness of the circumstances. To covenant with another is to make a pledge that lasts a lifetime.

In your early years, you have not enjoyed my efforts at promise keeping. A lot of my energy is directed at keeping you safe. This often frustrates you a great deal. You have trouble fathoming why the iron is not a toy because you see me "playing" with it so often.

The same dynamic plays out around knives. We regularly prepare food together as a family. You enjoy watching us cut up fruit, and because you are going to eat it, you want to dice your own strawberries and melons. We have seen you sneakily reach for a knife and then scream to the high heavens when we prevented you from picking it up. You experienced our denial as a deprivation. You were not capable of grasping that it is part of our promise to keep you safe.

There has been at least one moment where I failed miserably at that task. You were only a few months old. Your mom was venturing out with her friends for one of the first times since your birth. I was a solo parent for an evening. Recognizing through my keen sense of smell that your diaper was dirty, we headed towards the changing table. Things were so messy that the changing pad got soiled as well. I gently set you on the bed so I could clean everything up.

Then, I heard a thud followed by a scream. Turning around, I saw you on the floor wailing. I was so stunned that it took me a second to realize what was going on (and to this day I am still not sure how you managed to roll over because that was not yet in your repertoire).

I scooped you up and called your mom to meet me at the hospital. I drove there frantically while talking to my own mother and holding back tears. I worried about what was wrong and felt terrible for it happening under my watch.

Thankfully, you recovered quickly. By the time we arrived at the emergency room your crying had stopped. I think the medical staff found my alarm to be ridiculous, as there was little they could do for a child who looked quite healthy. I also learned that night that they do not, unless absolutely necessary, give young children CT scans because of the radiation involved. Doctors also make promises to keep us safe.

While all ended well, I still find myself reliving the emotions of that night from time to time. From the horror of knowing it could have been much worse if you had landed differently to an overwhelming sense of guilt for having failed in my duty as a dad, it was an experience that I never want to repeat. There is great pain in being the one that breaks a promise, even accidentally.

Sometimes that agony exists in keeping promises as well. We are currently engaged in a daily battle that commences every morning. It goes something like this:

> You: It's time to wake up!
>
> Mom: Let's get breakfast and then get ready for school.
>
> You: NOOOOO, I DON'T WANT TO GO TO SCHOOL!

Dropping you off at preschool involves a lot of emotional work for both of us. You cling to my leg until your teacher can coax you away. Then, you stand at the window to wave goodbye to me with a sad look on your face that silently screams, "Why are you leaving, daddy? Why?"

All of this pulls on my heartstrings more than you can know.

I desperately want what is best for you. That means working during the weekday so we have the resources to provide for your well-being now and in the future. That also involves leaving you to spend the day with other kids your age so you can develop social skills and learn new things.

You stare out the window desperately hoping I will change my mind. I pull out of the parking lot wanting nothing more than to turn the car around. Yet, doing anything else would be selfish in the long run despite the pain it causes us both in that instant.

This is a small example of the way promises can be costly. When rooted in love, they require us to put the needs of others before our own. We will make lots of promises to each other over the course of our lives. Here are three sacrificial ones that I made to you on the day you were born.

First, I promise always to act in your best interests, even if you are not able to see things that way.

This is the abstract version of the daycare dilemma. With every decision we make about your life—and how we share life together as a family—my intention is to start by considering what you need, to ask what is most beneficial for you. This assumes that your mom and I can always figure that out, which is unlikely. We are going to make mistakes, but they will never be caused by the wrong motivations.

I also recognize there are going to be times when you vehemently disagree with me. Those moments may even strain our relationship for a while. I am willing to suffer that cost if it means you are safer, healthier, and better able to thrive.

Here's a strange fact about me: I did not have my first drink of alcohol until my twenty-first birthday. I am not sure if that's due to great parenting, the influence of friends, my own personal morality, or some combination thereof. I do know that when my friends from high school returned home after our first year at college and had a different attitude towards alcohol, it proved to be the death knell of our relationship. They spent the summer binge drinking. I invested myself in more productive activities.

I already dread the thought of you being in similar situations. I worry about the pressures they will impose on you. You may experience my strict lines on these big questions as overly authoritarian, but my own experience has taught me the importance of navigating these formative years with a little extra caution until you are truly able to reflect on the choices you are making.

Paternalism has justifiably earned a bad reputation for the oppression it fosters. I have no desire to control your every move or to suppress all your freedoms, but I will always strive to put your long-term interests first, even if that means frustrating your immediate wants. I hope you will come to understand my motivations behind any acts of "tough love." Regardless, I will rest easy at night so long as I am confident that I spent the day putting you first.

Second, I promise to teach you what I know. This includes the lessons learned from my own mistakes.

Lots of people in the world come across as "know-it-alls." Others display a false modesty, not wanting to receive justly deserved accolades. I have tried to cultivate an accurate self-understanding—aware of my own talents, experiences, and accomplishments—but also humility about all that I do not know and cannot do.

You will need to find someone else to teach you about fishing and carpentry (ironic, since Jesus had these skills and I am supposed to know something about him). There is little I can teach you about basketball or art. My professional expertise is limited to religion and politics, which means I can teach you how to be an impolite dinner guest.

Beyond those subject areas, what I really want to teach you is a set of virtues. Indeed, I am writing you these letters because there is a way of being in the world that I hope you will find attractive and want to emulate. To the extent that I am successful, it is because I took Jesus's teachings to heart. Failures have usually resulted because I did not live out what I know to be true.

Humility and empathy are the places to start. "Fear of the Lord is the beginning of wisdom," declares the psalmist (111:10 NIV). I presume this is because beginning from a point of awe towards God reduces the time anyone spends in awe of themselves. Only when we minimize our own egos can we hear what others are saying, imagine what they are feeling, consider that our own judgments might be flawed, and learn of new possibilities. Taking in the perspectives of others and exploring new possibilities first requires setting aside our own self-importance.

I genuinely try, especially in difficult moments, to place myself in the shoes of others in an attempt to see things as they do. I try to act with intentions free of selfishness and malice. It regularly shocks me how many people, especially Christians, make no effort to hide their desire for vengeance or their pursuit of their own interests at great costs to others. The moments in life in which I have inflicted pain on others or served myself first are the places where regrets linger. I hope you too will see the value of these virtues because of the ways I have taught and modeled them for you.

Third, I promise to encourage your freedom and creativity in discovering who you are, what the world is like, and how you fit within it.

When you were "on the way" but before we knew your sex, people would ask if I was hoping for a boy or a girl. I struggled to form an answer. Either possibility promised a wonderful future. It seemed strange to be rooting for one over the other.

Behind the question seemed to be another. Did I want a son to raise to be just like me? A replica that would mirror my interests? Maybe even an attempt at achieving immortality through one's offspring? This last desire has never made sense to me. My great-great-great-great-great-grandchildren would never know, cherish, or celebrate me. My memory is just too distant for them.

All I want is for you to enjoy being you. Just as I found my own place in life that was radically different from my parents' paths, but very much supported by them, I want to offer you whatever assistance I can in finding what captivates and excites you, the passions that inspire you, and the dreams that motivate you.

With the exception of wanting you to know Jesus too, I come with no preconceptions. And if you struggle to connect with God in the same way, then that will also be a source of strength in our relationship, as we seek to understand each other better.

The world is a big place. Most of it is unfamiliar to me. It is also rapidly changing. A lot of what I once assumed with certainty is now held gently. It would be foolish for me to try and dictate your place within it. Rather than design a life for you, I am eager to walk beside you where I can and watch from afar where necessary, as you have your own experience of self-discovery.

I will say, though, that the early results are good. You are already rooting for my favorite baseball team. No doubt I exerted too much pressure there!

* * *

Going back at least to Aristotle, the keeping of promises is placed at the center of human virtue. Such moral expectations may overestimate the abilities of humans to follow through. After all, promises get broken all the time. I suspect this is less about people intentionally ignoring their obligations and more about people neglecting their commitments.

So, I will end this letter by making you one more promise: I will keep these vows to you front and center. I will be intentional about reminding myself of them. I hope you will hold me accountable to them.

Devotedly,

Dad

Dear Sons,

Growing up, I had hearing issues. I had tubes put into my ears more times than I can remember. I took hearing tests so many times that I had each of the variations memorized. One Thanksgiving, my new tubes got messed up and stuff started oozing out of my ears. As funny as it may sound, I got an ear infection from my baptism. In other words, that rebirth came with the same old ears. My ears have been a constant issue in my life. I still have moments when I struggle to get words to come out of my mouth.

Son, due to my hearing and speech issues, words have always been important to me. I place a great deal of weight upon the words that I share and take in.

Words matter. They create worlds. When I first held you, mere minutes after you were born, I whispered promises to you in the hospital nursery. It was just the two of us. In summation, I promised always to do my best in being your father. Each night, as you lie down to sleep, I repeat my promises to you. It is a reminder to you and, honestly, also to me.

I believe that it is important to return to these promises each day because we are always being formed. My hope is that these promises will form our bond as opposed to the cultural forces that seek to form men into machines that strive to dominate others. As the prophet Jeremiah contemplated centuries ago in the eighteenth chapter of his writing, we are always being formed and reformed as clay. We need to be aware of what is forming us. My aim in reciting these promises to you each day is that our relationship will be formed by them in an ongoing way.

The basis of my relationship with you is not your "success" or "performance." Our relationship is based upon promises. We see in the Hebrew Testament examples of promises or covenants in which each party agrees to a set of obligations towards the other. These covenants were actually based on ancient Near Eastern treaties between nations. Our relationship is more than a set of obligations towards each other. It is how we are going to be in relationship together —from the hospital nursery to my dying breath.

When people from the United States first landed on the Hawaiian islands, they met the native peoples there. The native Hawaiians would often go cheek to cheek with someone and breathe as a greeting. It is a beautiful custom that I learned about I completed my Clinical Pastoral Education on Oahu in 2005. Unfortunately, when people from the United States landed on the islands, they were not inclined to go cheek to cheek with a stranger and breathe. They would stick out their hands to shake the hands of the native Hawaiians, which was the typical greeting for them. Eventually, the native Hawaiians called these foreigners "haoles." The term is negative and is still used today. While doing my education there, I learned that the term means "without breath." For the native Hawaiians, the people who do not go cheek to cheek lack breath.

Son, from the first promise to the last, I have been cheek to cheek and sharing breath with you. Sometimes, it is in a nursery or on the floor before you go to sleep. Still, the intimacy of our relationship causes me to get cheek to cheek with you to remind you of who and whose you are.

Throughout your life, if you are willing, I promise to go cheek to cheek with you during times of struggle. I will say a word to you that sums up life for me: *ana-kephala-io-sas-thai*. It is a nineteen-letter word found in one of the longest run-on sentences that I have ever read (Ephesians 1:3–10). The author of Ephesians seems to be so excited to share this image of faith that he throws out all grammatical sense. Basically, the word means to put a new head on it. For me, it means that God can empower us to make the best out of the worst situations.

Recently, *anakephalaiosasthai* meant that when I got our family lost in the sands of Arches National Park, I was able to turn it into a teaching situation: Never go on a hike with a low phone battery! The word has also meant that when you fell and hurt your knee, we were able to learn about the dangers of jumping off the stairs for future reference. As Christians, it means that we have been able to take the image of the cross—a symbol of defeat, domination, oppression, and subjugation—and turn it into a symbol of victory, hope, triumph, and love. For me, this is what victory can look like in life.

I promise to teach you a life of *anakephalaiosasthai* because the world needs more men who are able to make the best out of the worst. It is what Joseph did when his brothers threw him into a pit in an effort to get rid of him, their father's favorite (Genesis 37). Most men would have sought revenge as soon as they had a chance. Instead, Joseph made the best out of the worst, which ultimately led him to saving thousands of lives in his former homeland, including those of his brothers. His courage enabled the rest of the story within which we can find ourselves today.

I do not know if I could have done what Joseph did in this story. Most expectations placed upon men are to be strong. For some, strong means to get revenge. For me, it means to be strong enough to be able to put a new head on a difficult situation. Because of Joseph's strength, he saved countless lives. He is a role model for me to follow in moments when life is gut-wrenching.

I promise to embody this type of strength when I am with you. I promise to try to instill this same way of being in you. I believe that countless lives are at stake if men cannot be strong in more constructive ways. I understand that this may sound as if it is some new age form of masculinity. Instead, I see it as an ancient way of living a godly life.

I have joked that if I ever get a tattoo it will be of *anakephalaiosasthai*. Sure, it is nice to put that message on my body, but it is better to express it in my actions. I promise to try to live a life in line with that of Joseph, Jesus, and countless other men who showed strength in ways that words fail to convey fully. It is a complicated way of understanding masculinity, but the world needs more men who can find their voice to be able to make the most out of the pits in which we sometimes find ourselves.

As I think about my next set of promises, I want to address a time when I struggled with words. As I shared previously, my first car was a 1971 Chevelle SS. Even though I was fourteen at the time of purchase, I noticed that the speaker covers in the car had Confederate flags on them. My reaction was that it was odd and that I wanted better speakers. If I had to do it over again, I would address the history of the Confederate flag and when it tends to show up in history. It was not that I was blind, but that I was quiet at a moment when I should have been clear.

I have learned that being silent in times of injustice is tantamount to siding with the oppressor. I am learning to find and own my voice in those moments. I promise to support you in finding your voice in those moments. I know that what is important to you will likely be different than it is for me. Fatherhood is not about forcing you to have the same commitments, but to encourage you to stand up for those commitments.

I heard one of your commitments as we were cheek to cheek one night reading *The Giving Tree*. In the story, a boy has a relationship with a tree. As the boy grows into a man, he needs more from the tree than simply apples or a tree swing. He ends up needing the tree to build a house and much more. Eventually, the only remaining part of the tree is the stump for the old man to sit on. I will never forget you screaming at the man not to cut the tree down in order to build a house. You yelled "No!" as your brother was trying to sleep in the other room. Your conviction, at age two, to care for creation was inspiring. I promise to support you in your commitment to care for creation even as we imagine a world where a tree tries to be a provider for a little boy.

When you were born, I found myself wrestling with the feeling that I needed to be a provider. I found myself trying to find side jobs in order to make more money. I worked even harder at my job at the time to ensure that I could still provide for you. Like many fathers, my initial attempts at providing were squarely focused on money.

I promise to be a provider for you in a variety of ways. In addition to finances, it also means that I will provide guidance on how to be successful at hide and go seek. I will provide curiosity when we have our weekly family worship time. I will provide for you in endless ways yet to be determined. I have many proverbial hats that I wear, but none is more important to me than being married to your mother and being your dad because you are both a source of endless joy.

I promise to love you completely for who you are. One of the most difficult situations that I see as a pastor are the times when parents and other family members fail to love someone for who they are—full stop, no strings attached. I have been with friends when they told their parents that they no longer wanted to be an engineer during the final year of college. Yikes! I have been with individuals when they came out to their parents as being gay. I was there to offer love, support, a hug, and resources when their parents kicked them out of the house and, worse, out of their lives.

Son, love can be embodied in many different ways. For example, once I was welcomed home as a prodigal son who did not deserve it at the time. This is true love. I have also experienced love with strings attached or with a desire to control and manipulate. For a season of my life, it destroyed me. Because I was devoted to that understanding of love, I lost countless friends. I could have lost many more if it were not for amazing grace. It is out of this experience that I promise always to love you fully. This is the love that I received from your mother. At first, it blew me away and it continues to do so. Your mother loved me in a way that changed my life. It is the kind of love that we read about in scripture, not a Hollywood script.

Son, promises shape relationships. Your mother and I exchanged promises on our wedding day. Those promises or vows frame our marriage. They are not so much a contract as a way of shaping the future that we seek to create together. Love is not how you feel about another person; it is how you make the other person feel about themselves.

We see promises in scripture as well. We use fancy language such as "covenant" for such promises, but in reality they are simply promises. Promises mattered back then just as they do today. We humans failed to hold up our end of the promises with God, yet we can still find ourselves "standing on the promises of God."

There may be times when I fail in these promises on my first try. Yet I will come back to these words because they frame our relationship. This is my first try at living my life. I am bound to mess up a few times. However, I will never forget the first time that I held you in the hospital nursery and the promises that I shared with you then. It was the first time that we shared breath. It was the beginning of a journey on which we would shape one another in countless ways.

Son, I may have cut your umbilical cord when you were born, but we will always be connected. We are connected not because of what one of us does or does not do. We are connected because of who we are. We do not have to do anything to form this relationship. It just is. Still, promises matter and I strive always to be a man of my word regardless of what life brings. Life brought me you and for that I echo the phrase that a father said to his prodigal son: "Son, you are always with me, and all that is mine is yours" (Luke 15:31 ESV).

With unbridled love and promises,

Dad

Notes for My Letter about Promises to Keep

8

Following Jesus

Dear Sons,

The biggest hurdles to your next spiritual experience are your previous spiritual experiences. Our possibilities in the future are often constrained by what has happened to us in the past. I know this has been true in my own encounters with God.

I grew up going to church. I went to the church preschool during the week and was in Sunday school most Sunday mornings. I did not want to be there. I would sneak out to get popsicles with a friend during worship. I confess that I made an inappropriate hand gesture out the window of the church van while on a youth group trip. Despite the love poured into me by this community, I did not fully comprehend what it meant to follow Jesus.

My path to finding Jesus involved climbing up the side of the mountain in California during the summer before I went into high school. My friend went one way down the mountain. I went another. His path had large rocks to grasp onto. My journey had pebbles and bushes. I ended up sliding down the side of the mountain, causing me to scream "Oh, God!" I continued to slide until I saw a bush. I grabbed onto it with all of my might. Just as in the Exodus story, where Moses needed a burning bush to be reassured of God's call on his life, I found myself being claimed by God in this small bush nestled amid the rocky mountain terrain. Resting there terrified, I heard God saying "I will hold you" as I clung to this unremarkable shrub that served as a source of divine provision. A few moments later, my friend came around the corner to help me as I slid down the remainder of the mountainside. I could not let go of the thought that my life had been held in God's hands.

Sons, at some points in your life, you will need to be held by God, family, and friends. Get used to it. And be ready to hold others. This is what it means to experience healing and helping others be healed, according to Jesus in Mark 2:1–12. In this story, a man who is paralyzed is carried to Jesus by his friends. Once there, Jesus heals this man because of his friend's faith. Many people think faith is personal and individualistic. Let me tell you there are times when all of us need to be carried by family and friends.

Later that summer, I went to church camp near Birmingham, Alabama. I woke up early one morning to watch the sunrise overlooking the lake from the mountaintop. I had a sense of overwhelming warmth and embrace. That moment, along with the aforementioned experience of falling down the mountainside in California, were my "finding Jesus" moments. A year later, at camp, I wrote myself a letter that I received nine months later. It arrived a few days before I gave my first sermon at my home church. The story of my call to ministry was unfolding and it was—as God says repeatedly in Genesis 1—"good."

Sons, when I experienced difficulty and turmoil in my life, I would often find ways to go back to this church camp, literally. I tried to relive my previous spiritual experiences by going back to the exact location where it occurred. It never worked. There was never that same warmth and embrace. I thought that I must have done something wrong because I knew where to sit, what to pray, but I never had that same experience. Sons, it took me numerous years, but I realized that a previous spiritual experience was getting in the way of my next one. I was trying to recreate what had been. Yet, it was nowhere close. The place was the same, but with new owners. Eventually, a developer bought the land from the YMCA. Now I would be trespassing, not on the property of the hospitable YMCA, but on the property of someone who was trying to make some money with that sacred piece of land. More importantly, the community was not there.

The people who loved me into being were no longer at the church camp. There was a diaspora after high school graduation. I had to find a new place and community in which to be formed. I was acting as many people did in the Bible. I wanted to recreate the past in the moments that required openness to new possibilities. Here is what I now *believe* to be true: Every mountain or valley or any other land feature can be holy. Holiness is about our relationship to a space and how we mark it. We do not need to be like Jesus and the woman at the well in John 4, who each came from communities who believed that they lived closer to God's one holy mountain. Furthermore, every community, small group, or prayer partner has the capacity to help us know who and whose we are. Please, do not let your most recent spiritual experience get in the way of the next because that mentality causes you to be stuck living in the past.

Sons, Jesus is always inviting us out of our tombs.

In 2015, I was a part of a small group of clergy from around the area who met twice a year. We were at a retreat center near Pasadena, California, that had the stations of the cross in life size experiences. It felt as if you were walking into the scene of biblical stories. I was struggling with my call to ministry at that time. During our day of silence, instead of going through the fourteen so-called stations of the cross which take one on the journey that Jesus took on the day of his crucifixion, including the falls, weeping, and crucifixion, I went straight for the last station—the empty tomb. Metaphorically, I had been living those other stations of the cross in my personal and professional life, I just wanted to be laid to rest. Circumstances in life can cause us to seek out renewal and rest, so I sat in the tomb from just after lunch to the dinner bell.

I sat in the tomb and cried. I felt as if I had "walked that lonesome valley" with Christ, as the hymn goes. Meanwhile, a colleague, unbeknownst to me at the time, walked the first thirteen stations of the cross, but was unable to find the tomb.

Sons, there will be moments when you feel as if you relate to various aspects of the stations of the cross. You might want to skip some parts of the story, but please know that following Jesus means that you do not have to experience excruciating pain, loss, and difficulty by yourself. There are always others walking alongside you. It is vital that we listen to and share our stories with others. It is in these moments that we better understand God's redemptive work in the world.

I serve in a Christian tradition that is skeptical, at times, of spiritual experiences. Perhaps, we are too rationalistic to be able to understand events that might seem too supernatural for some. I like that we value education, reason, and taking the Bible seriously, not literally. At times, I have been hesitant to share about the spiritual side of my life. My fear was that my tradition would see me as an outsider. I thought that I had to leave my tribe, but I kept being claimed by it. Sons, I have learned that a tribe is a community who celebrates and walks alongside you in your unfolding story. To follow Jesus, you need a community to walk alongside you, regardless of whether you find yourself doubting everything or on the side of a mountain.

As I came out of the tomb, I came upon a lush garden, saw resurrection in the bountiful garden as new life that broke the darkness of the ground, which I must have missed the first time passing through the area. The resurrection was waiting for me to come out of the tomb. It had been there all along. Just as Mary mistook Jesus as the gardener in the resurrection story of John's Gospel, I missed what had been waiting for me on the other side of the tomb. Sons, everyone needs help getting out of the tombs in which they find themselves. My hope and prayer is that you will always help people find the bountiful garden that they do not recognize. Sometimes, we need someone mistaken for a gardener to tell us this reality.

Throughout the gospels, we can read "you heard that it was said, but I tell you…" Each time I read these phrases, I think of all the ways that Jesus is telling this to me. Sons, you will often hear me say that "I used to think, but now…" This is not a statement of defeat. This is a statement of resurrection! It is in these moments that Jesus is inviting us to do midrash, which means to understand the stories of scripture better by playing with the "spaces" in between the words and letters to help bring the story to life. As your father, I cannot wait to do this with you as we play with scripture and with life in general. Further, I cannot wait for you to show me how I am set in my ways and invite me to think in a new way!

I grew up in the Bible Belt. I remember being impressed by other churches and their members being incredibly confident about their beliefs. They seemed to have the Bible memorized from cover to cover. I thought that unless I did the same I wouldn't be good enough to be a Christian, much less a pastor! Then, I realized that such memorization was usually a facade. Memorized bumper sticker phrases did not help when you were in a tomb. There was no depth to their actions. I have seen many of these same people who I idolized in high school for "knowing everything" no longer following Jesus once they walked that lonesome valley.

It is important to me that you walk alongside Jesus in a community who allows you to wrestle with all of your struggles, doubts, and questions. I hope that you will make space for others who need that same sense of community. In my experience, those aforementioned people who I idolized were some of the most inhospitable people who I have ever met. I wonder if they have actually met the Jesus whom I meet in scripture!

In August 2002, I woke up in a college dorm for the first time. I recall opening the door to find a young man collapsed in my door frame. My hunch was that he had gone wild the first time that he got an ounce of freedom. A few days later, I found out that I was correct. His parents were extremely protective. Therefore, when he had the chance, he tried everything as soon as possible. Later that day, I called my sister to say that we needed to buy our parents a weekend getaway somewhere because they "raised us right." Our parents allowed us room to learn, grow, and experience life.

Sons, I want to give you the space to do more than memorize Bible verses. I want you to experience much of the fun and beauty that life offers, so that one day you do not end up collapsed in the frame of a college dorm room. I have learned that following Jesus means staying a disciple. I will never be at your graduation ceremony when it comes to following Jesus. It does not exist. I have said that following Jesus is living a gerund phrase. Life is not simply about being saved (a one-time event), but about how God is always saving us (an ongoing relationship). We are supposed to keep asking questions and wrestling with God, as our spiritual ancestors did. Being a disciple means to stay a student of Jesus, especially when you think that you have it all figured out.

As you may learn about me, I change the lyrics of hymns and songs all the time. I do this to make them mine. For example, I do this with "Amazing Grace." It is not just a hymn for funerals. It is a hymn for discipleship. For this reason, I always change the line from "I once was blind, but now I see" to be "I once thought that I could see, but now I realize that I was blind." I have experienced (unknowingly most of the time) blind spots in my life. I thought that I had life all figured out and was doing it by the book. Then I realized that I was blind. However, as I take each step with Jesus, I am able to see, faintly, a little bit more, as Paul shares with the church in Corinth.

The only way to prevent spiritual blindness is to keep asking questions. We were made for such things. It goes all the way back to Adam and Eve. As the earliest scribes wrestled with this story, they wondered what it meant that Eve was made from Adam's side. The word in Hebrew that people translate as "rib" usually means "side." Some of the earliest people to wrestle with scripture pondered whether Adam and Eve were, actually, back to back, meaning they could not see each other until God separated them at their sides. God realized that Adam needed a helper, as did Eve. After naming all of the animals with God, Adam thought that he had it all figured out! Thanks to God, he realized that he was blind to almost half of what was around him. Adam needed someone else—Eve—to help him see his surroundings. I can relate to the experience of Adam being blind and then being able to see once he found others. We can only see within certain limits. I need others to help me see my blind spots. The sooner you realize this reality, the sooner you can follow Jesus properly.

In Christ's footsteps,

Dad

Dear Sons,

You were all loaded up in the car and our family was bound for Branson, Missouri. It was December, three short months after your birth, and we were nervous about how well you would travel on a long road trip. We asked your mom's parents to join us, as we were also concerned about being first-time parents so far away from home.

I posed a question to everyone as we headed out of town on our adventure. It was a thought experiment meant to stir up conversation and distract us from our worries.

"What do you think Jesse will be when he grows up?"

We spent miles debating our answers to this question. You were in the 7th percentile for height relative to other three-month-old children, so we quickly ruled out a basketball career. Instead, our responses varied from doctor to lawyer to professor to engineer.

You could dismiss these white collar suggestions as stemming from a lack of imagination, but actually they are far more revealing. We were a group of highly-educated professionals casting your future in our own image. Our dreams were projections of what we either once were or still hoped to be. They reflected the limitations of our vantage points. Our chosen paths prevented us from seeing you as a farmer living close to the soil or a welder skilled at using his hands.

These answers also disclosed something else. In that car, like many other places in our culture, we linked our identities to our work. So much of who we are is tied into what we do.

Evidence for this is found in articles about retirement which counsel folks dealing with the grief that comes from ending their career. Our jobs can be so fundamental to our sense of self that ceasing to work is equated with not being alive. Those who are not being paid to be productive are considered as good as dead. Thus, when I asked "What will Jesse be when he grows up?" we all assumed the question was related to the professional path you would pursue.

While our speculation was harmless, I have come to regret the question. The concern we had for your future focused on all the wrong things. My love for you is completely unrelated to whatever career you end up choosing. The last thing I would want is for you to believe my affection is connected to the job you hold, the degree you earn, or the status you reach. I love you because you are my son. Nothing else is required on your part.

That being said, I certainly hold hopes about how your life will unfold, but the most important one is not about where you work. My deepest desire is that you will come to know and follow Jesus, that your identity will be formed by being one of his disciples. I want you to experience what the Apostle Paul writes in 2 Corinthians when he says, "Therefore, if anyone is in Christ, the new creation has come. The old is gone, the new is here!" (5:17 NIV).

I write these words to you with significant trepidation. Lots of parents plead with God that their child will embrace the way of Jesus, but few bother to think about where it leads. Just listen to the invitation Jesus extends to his first followers in the Gospel of Luke: "Whoever wants to be my disciple must deny themselves and take up their cross daily and follow me. For whoever wants to save their life will lose it, but whoever loses their life for me will save it" (9:23–24 NIV).

Being a Christian is not reducible to a belief. Seeing Jesus only as a ticket to heaven ignores his message and ministry detailed in the gospels. The decision he demands from us is about making a commitment to a specific way of life. If we truly believe that Jesus is the Incarnation of God—the divine presence embodied in a human person—then we are compelled by that conviction to obey what he says, conform our actions to his teachings, and follow where he leads. To claim that Jesus is God's presence among us is to affirm that his example, exhortations, and expectations reveal the ways of God. Professing a faith in Jesus but refusing to take him seriously enough to change our lives accordingly is to make ourselves into fools by mocking God.

The way of life that Jesus invites us to choose is uncomfortable and costly. For Christians today, the cross is a positive symbol of our faith. We prominently hang it in our sanctuaries and wear it around our necks. We glorify the cross because of what we understand it to reveal about God's character and love. Yet to Jesus and his followers, the cross represented humiliation and agony. The Roman Empire reserved crucifixion as a punishment to shame and to torture insurrectionists simultaneously. Those who died in this painful way served as prominent examples of the consequences of challenging the Empire's oppression. The cross was a tool of torture to keep people in line.

So, when Jesus insists that his followers pick up their crosses, the meaning was not hard to miss. The path he invites them to walk down is one defined by sacrifice and self-denial. To choose to carry the cross is to join Jesus in a journey towards death.

That is not a message that resonates well in our contemporary culture. When the best seller lists are dominated by self-help books and similar messages are echoed in megachurch pulpits, the challenge presented by the cross is diminished. Ours is a consumerist era in which individuals' needs are paramount. The idea of being "countercultural" is overdone but when applied to Jesus' invitation to pick up our crosses the term proves apt. My prayer is that you will willingly choose obedience and faithfulness to this way, but you should be clear-eyed about what it entails.

When I headed off to college myself, I intended to become a psychiatrist. This appeared to offer the best of all worlds. I could simultaneously be of help to people and be compensated well for doing good. Psychiatry was an opportunity to live comfortably, perhaps even lavishly, and also to make a positive difference in the world.

Then, I took my first college course in biology. It was awful. Part of the problem was seeing how enthusiastic the professor was about the subject matter compared to how little I was interested in it. He raved about the Krebs cycle like I talk about baseball. Biology was an all-consuming passion for him.

I have never been more proud of a grade than the B+ I earned in that class. I was even more affirmed when I was among a small group of students he invited to serve as teaching assistants the following semester. However, I left the class certain that biology and other subjects in the hard sciences were not my cup of tea. The thought of spending a decade or more rigorously studying these topics as I progressed through college and medical school was depressing. There was no way I was going to become a doctor. That dream had become a nightmare.

This turned my world upside down. I may only have been eighteen years old but this plan had been animating my decisions for several years. I felt lost and directionless. Moreover, I had no idea where to turn for guidance.

So, I prayed.

I would like to claim this was the natural result of a deep spiritual life, but that would be a lie. My prayer life was not particularly robust as a teenager and could still use some work even now. Deciding to pray was an act of desperation. Not knowing what else to do, I did the conventional thing.

What happened soon after remains one of the stranger moments of my life. Indeed, it is so odd that I hesitate to share the story for fear you dismiss it. Still, this is what I experienced and how I interpreted what happened.

One afternoon, as I was going through this biology-induced vocational crisis, my roommate barged into our dorm suite and declared, "You have to see my parking spot!" Something as simple as parking a car is normally unremarkable but our dorm had been built in an area of campus that was largely devoid of parking. Most of the time this meant one had to park in a lot a couple blocks away and trek one's groceries a decent distance back to one's room.

However, there were a handful of spaces immediately behind that building that never seemed to open up. If you managed to snag one of those spots then you tried to go weeks without moving your car. Students would vigilantly monitor the spots and rush to move their cars if they saw one being vacated. It was objectively ridiculous but an entertaining part of our college lives.

As you can guess, my roommate had returned to campus and found one of these spots open. He immediately occupied it with his car. He was excited to find me in our suite so I could witness and celebrate his accomplishment. We walked over to the window to gaze upon his victory when I noticed the license plate of his Ford Taurus. It said "I TIM 412." Knowing that his parents were pastors, I recognized this was a reference to scripture. Being a biblically illiterate Christian, I had no idea what 1 Timothy 4:12 actually said. Upon being quizzed, my roommate was equally ignorant.

Dusting off my Bible, I opened it to 1 Timothy and read, "Don't let anyone look down on you because you are young, but set an example for the believers in speech, in conduct, in love, in faith and in purity." This instantly seemed like an answer to prayer. As I absorbed these words, I felt a sense of call. I was supposed to be a minister. Like a psychiatrist, that path promised the same chance to help people navigate the challenges of life. The only downside was it offered drastically less in terms of financial compensation. I felt tested. What mattered more to me? Was I more interested in helping people in times of crisis or accumulating wealth for myself? I followed God's call into ministry.

I like to joke about this episode by claiming that "following Jesus messed up my life." The well-off existence imagined by my teenage self was upended by an open parking spot. That inflection point led me to divinity school, to ordination, to serving Christ's church in various ways. It also took me into the messiness of people's lives, where I joined them in lament as they experienced tragedy and rejoiced with them in moments of profound ecstasy. The financial equation has worked out better than expected, but making money was never the motivation. Even at the most difficult points, I have felt this was work I am called to do and believe that undertaking has drawn closer to the heart of God. That has always left me grateful.

Still, it has involved sacrifices that extended far beyond money. Just as Jesus gave his life away on the cross for us, so the work of ministry often involves sacrificing yourself for others out of love. We seek to be nothing more and nothing less than imitators of Christ's example. I have strived, not always successfully, to lead a cross-shaped life.

Each of us who dares to accept Jesus' invitation has to determine how to respond faithfully. Your walk will look different than mine, and my own journey will certainly veer off in new directions. After all, Jesus himself never stayed in one place for long and apparently expects his followers to keep moving as well.

Despite our inability to know the places Jesus might ask us to go, I commend this costly, sacrificial, and uncomfortable way to you irrespective of these cautions. Following after him is easily the hardest thing I have ever done, but it is also the most rewarding way that I know.

This is the paradox disclosed in Luke's Gospel. By seeking to live only for ourselves, we end up losing our lives. Metaphorically, our self-absorption causes us to miss out on the richness derived from being oriented towards others. Metaphysically, Christians believe that our faith in Jesus opens up the possibility of redemption and eternal reconciliation with God in ways that we cannot achieve on our own. In choosing Jesus, we willingly die to ourselves only to discover the most abundant life that we can imagine.

Years ago, I stumbled across a decades-old column in *The Washington Post*. It told the amazing story of a guy in DC named Jermaine Washington. Just twenty-five years old at the time, Jermaine had struck up a friendship with a coworker—named Michelle Stevens—and they would often eat lunch together.

As they got to know each other, Michelle confessed to having lost all hope for her life. She had spent the last year on the transplant list waiting for a new kidney. She detailed the horrors of spending three hours a day, three times a week on a dialysis machine, and how her health was rapidly deteriorating. None of Michelle's family members and close friends were able or willing to be donors.

That is when Jermaine did something amazing. He spent four hours in surgery, let doctors make a twenty-inch incision into his body, and spent five days in the hospital, all for the privilege of donating one of his kidneys to his coworker and friend. It was the first friend-to-friend transplant performed at the Washington Hospital Center.

When asked why he was willing to endure such suffering, Jermaine simply stated, "I was watching my friend dying before my eyes. What was I supposed to do? Sit back and watch her die?" He was also asked where he found the courage to make such a sacrifice and said, "I prayed for it. I asked for God's guidance and that is what I got."

This inspiring story reveals the ways of Jesus at work. Motivated only by a sense of obedience to God's ways, and not by any obligation or financial incentive, this guy made a huge sacrifice that resulted in his friend finding new life. It would have been far easier for him to have merely sympathized with her circumstances or glibly promised to hold her in prayer. Instead, he put himself in the middle of a messy situation and did everything he could to ensure she would live.

That sounds a lot like what God was up to in the Incarnation. I also suspect that Jermaine would do it all over again because he discovered that the most meaningful way of being human is to give yourself away to others just like God has done through Jesus Christ for all of us.

While I promise to encourage and guide you, to teach you and serve as an example, my son, the decision on whether to turn your life over to Jesus is one that only you can make. Some people will dismiss it as silly. Others will profess such a commitment but fail to live it out. What I can tell you from my story and the stories of others like Jermaine is that those who take God seriously enough to give their lives away end up discovering more than they could ask or imagine.

In Christ,

Dad

Notes for My Letter about Following Jesus

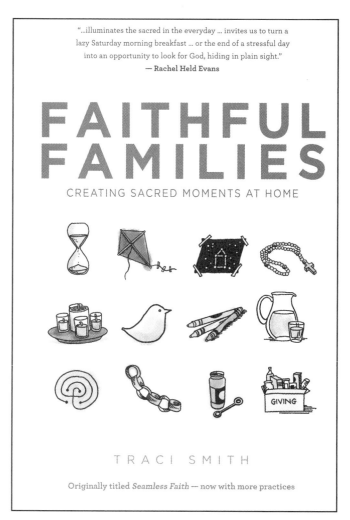